This is

HEROIN

Printed and bound in the UK by MPG Books, Bodmin

Published by Sanctuary Publishing Limited, Sanctuary House,
45–53 Sinclair Road, London W14 0NS, United Kingdom

www.sanctuarypublishing.com

Photo credits in order of appearance: 1. Lizzie Harper/Science Photo Library 2. Jerry Mason/Science Photo Library 3. Jerry Mason/Science Photo Library 4. Laguna Design/Science Photo Library 5. Garry Watson/Science Photo Library 6. PA Photos 7-12. Getty Images Inc 13. Alain Dex/Publiphoto Diffusion/Science Photo Library 14. Nigel Coke/Science Photo Library 15. Oscar Burriel/Science Photo Library 16. Cordelia Molloy/Science Photo Library 17. Sue Ford/Science Photo Library 18. Getty Images Inc 19. PA Photos 20. PA Photos 21. George Chin/Redferns 22. PA Photos 23. PA Photos 24. Jacques M Chenet/Corbis 25. David M Martin MD/Science Photo Library 26. David M Martin MD/Science Photo Library 27. PA Photos 28. PA Photos

While the publishers have made every reasonable effort to trace the copyright owners for any or all of the photographs in this book, there may be some omissions of credits, for which we apologize.

ISBN: 1-86074-424-9

This is
HEROIN

CONTENTS

INTRODUCTION

The United Nations International Drug Control Programme (UNDCP) estimates that the number of heroin users throughout the world is 9.8 million.

The world is in the grip of a frightening drug: heroin. Crime, poverty, dependency, death and destruction trail in its wake. Add the needle and spoon, and it's the modern equivalent of a skull and crossbones preying on society. Over a century's experience of fighting the drug has failed to kill or tame the pirate and heroin's stranglehold remains as tight in the 21st century as it was in the 20th.

The United Nations believes there is a worldwide heroin-using community of nearly 10 million people – more than the population of some countries. The drug has been outlawed for most of its life and abused almost since the day it was discovered in the late 19th century.

In every western country its use has grown considerably in the past few decades and the production of opium, the raw material used to manufacture heroin, has increased exponentially to meet demand. There's no question, heroin is here to stay.

...and it presents a massive problem. Heroin is made dangerous because it is traded by criminals and almost always misused. It is illegally supplied cut with myriad – and sometimes noxious – adulterants, and often used in harmful and unhygienic environments, causing problems for both user, society and governments. The latter picking up the bill for everything from soaring crime rates to spiralling healthcare costs.

The challenge facing the world's governments is how to deal with it. For most of its life, more and more prohibitive laws have been introduced to deal with heroin. But, as Prohibition in 1920s and 1930s America demonstrated, a total ban has largely served to entrench global drug cartels and create billions in funds for the criminal organizations that run them.

Society's obligations to provide education about heroin, prevent life-threatening temptation and treat chronic addiction became more sophisticated in the second half of the last century, with methadone programmes and advertising campaigns. Any successes have rarely been clear-cut, however, because heroin spins a complex web of issues and problems, and the pace of change around its orbit often outstripped the legislators and doctors; the moral climate shifted, new research revealed new problems, heroin supply increased, heroin prices dropped and purity levels improved.

This means that methods and tools for tackling the problem need to be continually adapted and reviewed. That's the difficult part – changing minds and policies that deal with heroin always poses tricky trade-offs and judgements about their impact, essentially because it is the young who are most at risk.

But, by the 1990s, that radical sea change had begun to take place. A more enlightened, better-managed and better-financed approach to the problem was adopted by several countries. Some European governments and a number of other western countries, notably Australia, began to take harm-reduction issues more seriously. Treatment, not punishment, became the new watchword.

The speed of this change was clearly demonstrated by the UK's experience. In 1998 its first 'drugs tsar', Keith Hellawell, unveiled a ten-year drugs strategy based around young people, communities, treatment and availability, and setting major long-term targets: to cut heroin use by 25 per cent in 2003 and, by 2008, halve its use, reduce its availability by 50 per cent and double the number of heroin abusers in treatment.

By 2001 some of these targets were believed to be unachievable; Hellawell's role as anti-drugs coordinator had been sidelined; and, although his strategy template was still being applied, it was under review. It appeared that the problem of heroin was beginning to be seen more as a public health issue than a criminal one.

In 2002 UK police chiefs broke new ground by recommending that heroin users be sent for treatment rather than prosecuted, and the reintroduction of widespread prescription of heroin was being examined by a Home Affairs Select Committee and the UK's National Treatment Agency.

Further, a former UK cabinet minister and a serving police chief added their voices to the pro-legalization of heroin lobby, which seeks to break the drug's link with crime and to hand governments a sizeable income from taxing the legal sale of it. It is argued that these funds, potentially worth millions, can then be used for addiction treatment or prevention.

However, after more than a century of living with heroin and its associated problems, it is clear that there are no easy solutions. Complete prohibition hasn't worked, yet legalization of heroin or even decriminalization remain distant, and bring with them their own problems of control and increased demand.

As countries, their governments and their populations become more mature and sophisticated with regard to their perceptions of the drug and its use, politicians and experts will continue to weigh the evidence for an overhaul of drug laws, and examine and test new techniques for dealing with heroin. In the meantime, the drug's hold remains firm.

CULTURE

'Junk is a one-way street.' - William Seward Burroughs

HEROIN IS HEADLINE NEWS

The impact of drugs on modern media and culture has been enormous. Drugs are rarely off the news agenda. There are drugs books, drugs films, drugs plays, drugs songs, even fashion spreads have fallen under the spell of illegal narcotics. All that is needed now is *Drugs: The Musical* and every cultural base will have been covered.

Arguably, though, heroin has had more success than any other at imprinting its bewitching power on to the cultural consciousness. All illicit drugs provide their highs, occasionally, they can create serious health problems and, sometimes, they may even kill. But heroin regularly delivers all three outcomes and has the capacity, like no other drug, to destroy lives and lead to tragedy. This has given it the status of public enemy number one and – because bad news sells – the power to dominate news bulletins, whip up media frenzies and guarantee increased newspaper sales and better ratings on TV and radio. Consequently, the media is fascinated by heroin. The public fear it. And politicians make capital from it.

As the 20th century turned into the 21st, there was no let-up. In fact, heroin was filling increased acres of newsprint and giving anxious leader writers more opportunities to warn of the drug's perils. Because it creates so many social and health problems – the vast majority of drug treatment resources are aimed at opiate and heroin users – there are myriad different angles for journalists and commentators to spin from it.

Literally any story, from teenage delinquency to illegal immigrants, can be written around heroin – and they are: 'Glamorous Life of Ex-Model Ended in Drug Squalor'; 'When Heroin Touches an Entire Town'; 'Opium Protesters Attack Refugees'; 'MI5 Fears Flood of Afghan Heroin'; 'Anti Drug Shock Tactics'; 'Girl, 13, on Heroin Charge'. These headlines have already been written and there are thousands of similar ones waiting to be. This is because newspaper editors can always fall back on heroin deaths to create that day's splash story.

Thus, in 1997 the drug was rarely off the front page of US tabloids and the leader position in radio broadcasts when the leafy Texas town of Plano was haunted by a string of heroin overdoses. Suddenly, the drug's presence in the affluent, gated community alerted dozens of other sleepy, white picket-fenced Pleasantvilles from Baltimore to Florida that the menace was in their midst. America was put on notice that heroin-related deaths in the country had more than doubled since the beginning of the 1990s.

And after being the top bulletin on TV news it doesn't take long for heroin to pass from the news media to the entertainment industry. Just five years later the Plano tragedy would inspire US director Stephen Kay when he came to shoot the film *Wasted* (see the section on 'Heroin movies' on page 27).

RACHEL WHITEAR

In Britain another banner headline, 'This Is How Heroin Killed Our Girl', in March 2002, reminded everyone that the drug doesn't discriminate. Heroin can touch those from the most affluent homes and with the most potential, making their descent even more painful to witness. Beneath the headline were two pictures of the same girl, Rachel Whitear. One showed Rachel dressed in her school uniform; the other was a harrowing colour shot of Rachel dead. The 21-year-old university dropout had been found on her knees, slumped on the floor of a bedsit, a hypodermic syringe still clasped in her hand. She had been dead three days.

Rachel's sad and lonely death made the front pages of every newspaper and it was the top story on TV and radio news programmes for a week despite the fact that it had taken place two years previously. What made this death front-page news was that Rachel's stepfather and mother allowed police photographs of their daughter's blackened, bloated and bloodied body lying in the seaside slum to be used in an anti-heroin video shown to schoolchildren and partly financed by the government. (See the section on 'Effective Heroin Prevention' on p133.)

THE TWIN EVILS: HEROIN AND TERRORISM

The 11 September terrorist attacks on New York also had the effect of reinforcing heroin's media profile as the ultimate evil. US President George W Bush didn't hesitate to link heroin with the 21st century's first big battle: the war against terror. The drug was perceived as an ally of Osama bin Laden's al-Qaeda terrorists and the Taliban regime, which ruled Afghanistan until its overthrow in late 2001.

By destroying the Taliban, Bush pledged, the USA would hit Afghanistan's lucrative heroin market hard. In his address to the UN General Assembly in November 2001 he said, 'I make this promise to all the victims of that regime: the Taliban's days of harbouring terrorists and dealing in heroin and brutalizing women are drawing to a close.'

HEROIN CHIC

Although ubiquitous, heroin's success at permeating the media and culture has been bolstered by its ability to reinvent itself and add new layers to its myth. This was most notable in the early 1990s. Prior to then, heroin's brooding influence was largely as part of the counter-culture. It was perceived by most as a drug for losers – Wall Street winners used cocaine.

Then the fashion pack adopted the drug and a new paradigm kicked in. Images of junkie losers with dirty needles in filthy squats were replaced with scenes of bone thin, sexy models in filthy squats. Heroin wasn't just dangerous, it was cool. And once it made it on to glossy double-page fashion spreads it soon passed from the underground to the mainstream. Wall Street brokers traded their coke spoons for smack spikes.

Dubbed 'heroin chic', photographers like Corinne Day, David Sims, and

Juergen Teller shot fashion spreads against seedy backdrops with models who appeared strung out, their dark-rimmed, sunken eyes reflecting an elegantly wasted look.

Adverts for everything from computers to cars eschewed wholesome, radiantly healthy supermodels with perfect glowing skin for painfully thin models with hollow eyes starring listlessly from posters and magazines. It was, argued the style magazines at the time, a rebellion against the phony airbrushed images associated with fashion.

However, it was a commercial decision too. Stick-thin models posing in stupor-like states and surrounded by drug paraphernalia were suddenly in vogue – and it sold products. James King – now an actress, who appeared in the 2001 blockbuster *Pearl Harbor* – was famously photographed in 1997 by the young fashion photographer Davide Sorrenti. The teenager was slumped on a sofa, cigarette clasped between fingers and picking at the holes in her tights. On the wall were pictures of dead junkie punk icon Sid Vicious and a sweet-looking Kurt Cobain, his own self-inflicted death recalled by the dateline on the poster: 1967–1994.

'We've seen reports that many of our fashion leaders are now admitting – and I honour them for doing this – they're admitting flat out that images projected in fashion shoots in the last few years have made heroin addiction seem glamorous and sexy and cool. And as some of those people in those images start to die now, it has become obvious that that is not true. You do not need to glamorize addiction to sell clothes.' - Bill Clinton, former US President

The model from Nebraska said she was 14 when she was first offered heroin and hooked by the time she was 16. 'I was surrounded by drug abuse,' she said, adding that it was almost natural because all her peers, the photographers and magazine editors appeared to be doing drugs: 'It was something that was always there.' When more commercial photographers started copying the style for high-profile ad campaigns, the look went mainstream.

It was as if everyone was injecting, snorting or smoking the drug, and media culture came to reflect this. Sorrenti's fatal overdose in 1997, at the age of 20, was a jolt for the fashionistas and finally blew the lid off the industry's affair with heroin. Everyone knew people who were jacking up behind the scenes, but the extent of heroin use was a closely guarded secret – models and photographers closed ranks over their light-boxes. Sorrenti's death and the impassioned anti-heroin statements by his brother and mother brought the dangers of the drug into the public arena.

Heroin wasn't, however, just another cosmetic image manufactured by stylists and photographers – it was something that killed and it was cutting a swathe through the beautiful people. By the time of Sorrenti's death, King's own fashionable listlessness wasn't something that had to be created by an imaginative make-up artist – she was displaying all the hallmarks of heroin abuse for real. And it wasn't a pretty sight.

The dangers of a heroin epidemic being unleashed were recognized by former US President Bill Clinton when he attacked the fashion industry for popularizing heroin chic in May 1997. Taking his lead from Sorrenti's death and admissions from some magazine editors that the wasted look had glamorized heroin use, Clinton said, 'They [fashion leaders] are admitting flat out that images projected in fashion shoots in the last few years have made heroin addiction seem glamorous and sexy and cool. And as some of those people in those images start to die now, it has become obvious that that is not true. You do not need to glamorize addiction to sell clothes.' Clinton also called the glorification of heroin 'destructive' and continued, 'It's not beautiful. It is ugly. And this is not about art. It's about life and death. And glorifying death is not good for any society.'

As one of the architects of the heroin chic look, Sorrenti's death also prompted newspaper leader writers to tackle the link between heroin and celebrity. Ironically, though, the media's fascination with fame and illegal behaviour only further glamorized the drug as a lifestyle accessory to be acquired along with a Prada handbag.

The fact that the rich and the famous were using heroin gave editors the opportunity – and excuse – to fill their pages with pouting photographs of models and actors, which compounded the link between heroin and fame. Heroin had acquired a new image, far away from dirty needles and

Illustration of a flowering opium poppy, *Papaver somniferum*. The flower contains a yellow starfish-like stigma. When the petals fall, the stigma and carpel (capsule) are left (UPPER CENTRE). The carpel contains young seeds. It is from the sap of these unripe capsules that crude opium is harvested, containing numerous alkaloids including morphine, heroin, and codeine. It is used medically as a sedative, an analgesic, and extensively as a narcotic drug, forming dependency at an early stage.

Opium poppy flowers. Opium can be refined to yield pure heroin, which induces feelings of warmth and euphoria. Frequent use leads to tolerance and addiction.

Seed heads of the opium poppy. One carpel is sectioned to reveal its seeds.

hookers in dark alleys. Stars used it. The entertainment industry feted it. This was celebrity endorsement – always a powerful cocktail and a guarantee that others would follow.

Clinton's assertion that heroin has no place in society's cultural development is wishful thinking. Heroin use has escalated and its cultural influence is more prevalent than it has ever been. It's possible to put together a whole heroin-themed jukebox, starting out by slipping Alice In Chains' 'Junkhead' or The Velvet Underground's 'Heroin' out of the CD collection.

Even the local cinema could mount a smack retrospective, kicking off with the double bill *Requiem For A Dream* followed by *French Connection II*. And for a heroin read, library shelves are literally groaning under the weight of all the literature – Irvine Welsh's *Trainspotting*, Luke Davies' *Candy* or practically anything from William Burroughs – celebrating the drug.

Now that heroin's dangerous glamour is mainstream and its controversial stature has been recognized for green lighting movies and selling everything from T-shirts to the latest chart hit, it will continue to be a fertile seam mined by film-makers, musicians, artists and writers who have outgrown the traditional demons of booze and coke. That means more heroin songs, more heroin films and more heroin books. In the meantime, someone is probably writing that heroin musical right now.

HEROIN MOVIES

'*Requiem For A Dream is not about heroin or about drugs. In fact, I was never interested in making a movie about junkies – I find junkies really boring and uninteresting.*' – Darren Aronofsky, director of *Requiem For A Dream*

In 1916 the movie magazine *Variety* proclaimed 'there is nothing left' for the drug film. It was wrong. Since the first US-produced dope film, 1894's kinescope *Opium Joint* (aka *Chinese Opium Den*), there has been a steady stream of movies with drugs playing a supporting role. More recently, heroin has become a bona fide star.

A 1997 study of movie rentals in the USA found that 22 per cent of the 200 most popular films depicted illicit drugs and about a quarter of those (26 per cent) contained graphic portrayals of their preparation and use. Also, surprisingly, very few (15 per cent) contained an anti-drug message.

For the most part, directors working in the first half-century of film were not interested in issues like

There are now more than 200,000 heroin users in Britain, compared with little more than 1,000 registered users in the 1970s.

accuracy. Drugs – heroin and opium in particular – were the dramatic props and realism only had a walk-on part. Indeed many of the early movies, which featured heroin or opium, mostly addressed the moral hysteria that surrounded the drugs rather than the users or narcotics themselves. First and foremost the films were designed to warn, sometimes entertain.

In the very early years of cinema, drug use and the possession of narcotics were not legislated upon and an opium user or heroin addict didn't carry the moral stigma they do today. This meant a crop of US and European movies set in opium dens – such the 1906 French film *Rêves D'Un Fumeur D'Opium* ('The Opium Smoker's Dreams') – played in theatres before legislation and changing social attitudes dictated a new agenda in Hollywood.

The introduction of the 1909 Opium Exclusion Act, which ended the legal importation of opium into the USA, had some effect in reining in the appearance of drugs. However, many films, such as 1908's *The Energizer* and 1912's *For His Son*, continued to employ morphine and opium plots by featuring the legal medicines that contained these narcotics.

By the time the Harrison Narcotics Act was passed in 1914, the tone of the morphine (or heroin) film had changed. *The Secret Sin*, released in 1915, and 1916's *The Devil's Needle* warned of the harsh realities addicts faced. These moral tales were not, however, absorbed by Hollywood itself. The silent movie stars, directors and producers had dropped opium as their drug of choice and were now injecting heroin or morphine. It didn't take long for one of the first film industry casualties to be racked up. In 1923 the morphine-addicted Wallace Reid died, aged just 31. This prompted his wife, the film star Florence, to mount a second career as a crusader against drugs, culminating in her campaigning exposé *Human Wreckage*.

The first attempt to curb the proliferation of heroin and morphine in film came in October 1927. In an attempt to stave off rigorous censorship, the Motion Picture Association agreed to endorse and boycott a list of 36 controversial subjects drawn up by Will Hays. The use of drugs and drug trafficking were listed near the top of this list. This was reinforced by the 1930 Motion Picture Production Code, which prohibited any mention of addiction or trafficking on screen. This gave the Production Code Administration (PCA) a licence to deny a seal of approval to any film that broke the code, effectively dooming its release.

For the next two decades sex not drugs occupied the moral guardians. Then, in 1955, Otto Preminger's *The Man With The Golden Arm* blasted apart the taboo surrounding narcotics abuse, with Frank Sinatra portraying heroin addict jazz drummer, Frankie Machine. The film was in violation of the PCA, which refused to grant it a certificate, however Preminger released the film himself. Its success helped convince the PCA to amend its code a year later to allow treatments of drug addiction. Although the audience never gets to see the needle in Sinatra's arm he is seen preparing to tie off a tourniquet and the camera lingers on his face as the rush hits. Heroin had become a major movie star.

This episode seemed to set the pattern for the next few decades. Although the 1997 movie survey shows that marijuana and cocaine have appeared more frequently (51 per cent and 33 per cent respectively) in films than heroin, they have often been merely the backdrop – something smoked or snorted by a cast of sleazy characters. Few cocaine films have also actually dealt with the character's addiction. Most, like *Scarface* or *Blow*, were content to use the drug as the commodity producers and suppliers fought over. Only very few, such as *The Boost* and *Bright Lights, Big City*, concentrated on the user and his problems.

However, heroin, which was depicted in 12 per cent of the movies surveyed in 1997, often took the central role and, since the early 1970s, smack movies have been packing them in. In 1970 Paul Morrissey's *Trash* featured the first shot of needle puncturing skin. But it was 1971 that was to herald a turning point for the drug; in that year no fewer than four mainstream heroin movies were screened. *Jennifer On My Mind* was released alongside *Born To Win* (aka *Addict*), starring George Segal, *The Panic In Needle Park*, which made Al Pacino's reputation as an actor, and Floyd Mutrux's *Dusty And Sweets McGee*. The latter featured a character getting a fix under his tongue and, like many early heroin movies, did not stack the screen with authority figures expressing their moral outrage about the drug.

As plentiful supplies of cheap heroin began to wash on to US streets, a cinematic response also arrived, via blaxploitation flicks and big-budget thrillers. The best known is 1971's *French Connection*, filmed in New York and heroin's key trafficking point of the time, the French port of Marseille. Its sequel, 1975's *French Connection II*, was shot almost entirely in France and featured Gene Hackman's character Popeye Doyle experiencing the agonies of cold turkey.

The 1980s saw a shift of emphasis to concentrate on real-life casualties: punk's best-known heroin abuser Sid Vicious featured in Alex Cox's 1986 biopic *Sid And Nancy*, Charlie Parker was Clint Eastwood's subject in the jazz-tinged *Bird,* and Chet Baker's slide from James Dean lookalike to wretched smack trumpeter was captured by photographer Bruce Weber in his 1988 documentary *Let's Get Lost*.

Then at the end of that decade, in 1989, Gus Van Sant established the cinematic vocabulary and visual template of the contemporary heroin movie with *Drugstore Cowboy*. In this film, set in the 1960s, the actors Matt Dillon, Heather Graham, and Kelly Lynch raid pharmacies and do any and every drug they steal with vivid visual point-of-view angles – blurred vision, dead-fish gaze, spinning, dizzy – providing the audience with an inside taste of the drugs' dramatic effects. A cameo appearance by *Junky* author William Burroughs as a drug addict priest seals the heroin angle.

Heroin's ability to sell cinema tickets was emphasized by *Drugstore Cowboy*. And now, as audiences become more immune to violence, sex and drugs, film-makers realise that an injection of smack into a movie script will always fill seats. This is because heroin has many more appealing elements for screenwriters and directors than do many other narcotics. As far as modern movies go, marijuana is just a high-school giggle; everyone has had a puff. But heroin is dangerous. It establishes an immediate, albeit predictable, character arc and, although often clichéd and well visited, the plot line will have easily definable, strong turning points: good-looking character has it all, or at least something; he/she is introduced to smack and then seduced by it; he/she loses control as the descent into addiction takes over. This introduces the possibility of creating a very romantic anti-hero and gives directors a licence to visit unimaginable horrors on the character as they are sucked further in by the drug and the low-life subculture surrounding it. Audiences see the normal side of life every day, but heroin culture allows them to walk on the wild side for 90 minutes or so.

The end scene of a heroin film is equally powerful, offering up tragedy or redemption. Depending on the moral and philosophical tone of the director there will be death or a life rebuilt after cold turkey. By the final frame, the heroin movie will usually also have taken unreasonably beautiful leading actors and destroyed them.

Visually, what also gives heroin the drop on other drugs is that it isn't simply snorted, smoked or swallowed. There is the whole shocking paraphernalia of the junkie: the syringes, the belts for tying off, the cotton wool and spoon are all perfect props for the cinematographer to shoot in close up. The act of injecting is much more visually shocking than popping an E. The syringe will break skin and then fill with blood as it hits a vein. It'll also leave the film's character with lasting physical effects and he will wear these track marks and scabs like battle scars as the movie draws to its climax.

Moreover, heroin wasn't just appearing in films. Real-life Hollywood stars had come to embrace the drug. River Phoenix, who played a junkie hustler in Van Sant's *My Own Private Idaho*, died in 1993, aged 23. His premature death was given a twist of celebrity sleaze when it was discovered that he had collapsed outside the hip Viper Room club, off LA's Sunset Boulevard and owned by movie star Johnny Depp. Blood tests from Phoenix's autopsy report verified the presence in the actor's blood of alcohol, Valium, heroin, and cocaine - the last two being the vital ingredients of a speedball.

A few years later, Robert Downey Jr, an Oscar nominee for his portrayal of Charlie Chaplin, fought a public battle against heroin and other drug addictions, culminating in rehab and a prison sentence on the back of narcotic and weapons charges. And then in a move that demonstrates how art imitates life, in 2002 Phoenix's sister Summer turned up in her own Hollywood heroin vehicle, *Wasted*. Based on the real-life story of the heroin-related deaths of 17 kids in a Texas town, Summer admitted that the film stirred up the death of her brother and that her mother was pleased that at least her character survived. 'My mother would have disowned me had she died,' she said. 'It's all too close to reality.'

Heroin chic, increased purity and bumper crops of opium have extended the 'reel life' of the heroin movie into the 21st century and it's more than likely that a script featuring the drug is already waiting for the green light on a producer's desk. Opening shot: 'In a darkened room, Jack cranks up his works and shoots up...'

HEROIN'S STARRING ROLE IN FILMS

THE DEVIL'S NEEDLE (1916, DIR CHESTER WITHEY)
The film that *Variety* believed would put the final nail in the coffin of drug films because they had become so commonplace. An artist, played by Tully Marshall, and his muse, Norma Talmadge, become hooked on morphine. They manage to beat their addictions through will-power and – incredibly – hard work on a farm.

NARCOTIC (1932, DIR DWAIN ESPER)
Doctor becomes hooked on heroin following a car accident that puts him in hospital.

THE MAN WITH THE GOLDEN ARM (1955, DIR OTTO PREMINGER)
Starring Frank Sinatra and based on the book by Nelson Algren, the first film in the sound era to deal explicitly with heroin addiction. Also featured a Saul Bass title sequence and an Elmer Bernstein score, but was refused a certificate by the US ratings board on release.

A HATFUL OF RAIN (1957, DIR FRED ZINNEMANN)
A soldier becomes hooked on drugs following a war injury and struggles to keep his addiction hidden.

SYNANON (1965, DIR RICHARD QUINE)
Gritty drama about addicts trying to kick their habit in rehab. Stars Chuck Connors, Richard Conte, and Eartha Kitt.

TRASH (1970, DIR PAUL MORRISSEY)
Joe Dallesdandro plays the junkie in this gritty, authentic film, cruising the Lower East Side for another fix and passing through a dozen squalid sexual encounters. Holly Woodlawn acts as his lover-protector. Thought to be the first film to graphically show a needle breaking skin followed by a shot of heroin.

THE PANIC IN NEEDLE PARK (1971, DIR JERRY SCHATZBERG)
The film that made the reputation of Al Pacino, based in a community of users. Abandoned after an illegal abortion, Helen played by Kitty Winn falls in with small-time drug dealer Bobby, played by Pacino. She slowly learns about the world of heroin as they deal drugs and steal. Bobby graduates from occasional use – chipping – to become a full-time addict. Also stars Raul Julia and Paul Sorvino.

JENNIFER ON MY MIND (1971, DIR NOEL BLACK)
Written by Erich Segal, this drama follows Michael Brandon through Europe where he meets Tippy Walker, playing Jenny. They both try marijuana, but Jenny graduates to heroin.

BORN TO WIN (AKA ADDICT) (1971, DIR IVAN PASSER)
Starring George Segal as JJ, a Manhattan hair stylist whose addiction to heroin leads him into trouble when he rips off the mob. Robert De Niro plays a cop on JJ's tail.

DUSTY AND SWEETS McGEE (1971, DIR FLOYD MUTRUX)
Cinema verité with a cast including strung-out junkies playing themselves and Billy Gray of TV's *Father Knows Best*. Gray plays a narc against the cityscapes of Los Angeles and the film features a fix that involves injecting a needle under the tongue.

FRENCH CONNECTION (1971, DIR WILLIAM FRIEDKIN)
Gene Hackman attempts to crack an international drug ring masterminded by a French gang. The opening shots are of Marseille, the French port through which large quantities of illegal heroin passed in the 1970s.

FRENCH CONNECTION II (1975, DIR JOHN FRANKENHEIMER)
Shot on location in France, Gene Hackman chases Fernando Rey, who plays a Marseille drug lord. Features Hackman in the definitive movie cold turkey scene.

MIDNIGHT EXPRESS (1978, DIR ALAN PARKER)
A young American is arrested in Turkey for smuggling heroin and sent to a hellish Turkish prison. Stars Brad Davis and John Hurt.

CHRISTIANE F (1981, DIR, ULRICH EDEL)
Based on the autobiographical account of a 13-year-old Berlin girl's heroin addiction, set to a soundtrack by David Bowie.

LIQUID SKY (1982, DIR SLAVA TSUKERMAN)
Aliens visit New York and prey on a bunch of Lower East Side junkies.

SID AND NANCY (1986, DIR ALEX COX)
An account of the life and death of punk rock's best-known heroin casualties, Sex Pistols bassist Sid Vicious and his American groupie girlfriend Nancy Spungen. It was alleged by former New York Doll Jerry Nolan that Nancy was the first junkie to turn Vicious on to heroin.

LET'S GET LOST (1988, DIR BRUCE WEBER)
Just before this documentary about his life, heroin addict Chet Baker fell from the window of an Amsterdam hotel.

BIRD (1988, DIR CLINT EASTWOOD)
Starring Forest Whitaker in the main role of heroin addict and saxophonist Charlie Parker.

DRUGSTORE COWBOY (1989, DIR GUS VAN SANT)
Stars Matt Dillon, Kelly Lynch, and Heather Graham raid pharmacies for every type of drug available in the late 1960s. Includes a cameo from writer William Burroughs.

NAKED LUNCH (1991, DIR DAVID CRONENBERG)
Although the film's protagonist is hooked on the bug spray he uses, this is an adaptation of the book by junkie beat writer William Burroughs.

H (1991, DIR DARRELL WASYK)
A harrowing weekend during which two heroin addicts attempt to beat their habit by boarding themselves inside their apartment.

RUSH (1991, DIR LILI FINI ZANUCK)
Jennifer Jason Leigh and Jason Patric star in this movie about undercover cops who shoot up to prove their credentials and end up as addicted, scab-covered, emaciated junkies.

MY OWN PRIVATE IDAHO (1993, DIR GUS VAN SANT)
Keanu Reeves slums it with junkie street hustler River Phoenix, whose own cinema career was ended prematurely later the same year when he overdosed on a heroin-based drug cocktail.

PULP FICTION (1994, DIR QUENTIN TARANTINO)
Starring Uma Thurman and John Travolta, the latter's acting career was resurrected after playing a junkie hitman in Tarantino's follow-up to *Reservoir Dogs*. Mistaking Travolta's heroin for coke, Uma Thurman's character snorts an almost fatal dose.

KILLING ZOE (1994, DIR ROGER AVARY)
Eric Stoltz is American safecracker Zed, called to Paris by crime partner Eric (played by Jean-Hughes Anglade) to rob a bank on Bastille Day. However, the heist goes wrong and Anglade turns against Stoltz and his girlfriend Julie Delpy (the Zoe of the title) in a heroin-induced frenzy.

THE BASKETBALL DIARIES (1995, DIR SCOTT KALVERT)
Adaptation of Jim Carroll's cult novel of the same name, starring Mark Wahlberg and Leonardo DiCaprio as heroin buddies.

THE ADDICTION (1995, DIR ABEL FERRARA)
Explores the more metaphysical questions of needle culture with a vampire who mainlines blood like heroin.

TRAINSPOTTING (1995, DIR DANNY BOYLE)
Ewan McGregor and Jonnie Lee Miller and their shoot-up buddies on a Scottish estate put their looks at risk in this comic, gritty film based on the book by Irvine Welsh. McGregor stars as Renton, who spends much of his life getting high and stealing money to support his habit. Miller plays Sick Boy with Ewen Bremmer as Spud.

BASQUIAT (1996, DIR JULIAN SCHNABEL)
Aged 19, Jean Michel Basquiat was a graffiti artist. Eight years later, in 1988, he was one of the most acclaimed painters in the art world and also hooked on heroin. His addiction eventually led to the death of the self-destructive artist played by Jeffrey Wright. David Bowie plays artist Andy Warhol.

GRIDLOCK'D (1997, DIR VONDIE CURTIS-HALL)
Tupac Shakur, Thandie Newton, and Tim Roth are users trying to go straight.

TU AS CRIE: LET ME GO (1997, DIR ANNE CLAIRE POIRIER)
A mother, whose 26-year-old daughter was murdered while working as a heroin-addicted prostitute, explores their relationship in this Canadian documentary. Features interviews with current and former heroin addicts, doctors and drugs workers.

PERMANENT MIDNIGHT (1998, DIR DAVID VELOZ)
An adaptation of TV scriptwriter Jerry Stahl's autobiographical account of how he blew a fortune on smack. In the opening scene a strung-out Ben Stiller (playing Stahl) pumps his arms to accentuate a vein, loads his

system with heroin, and collapses. He also shoots up in his jugular for a quicker high.

HIGH ART (1998, DIR LISA CHOLODENKO)

Revolves around the heroin problem of photographer Lucy Berliner, played by Ally Sheedy. However, the drug is only snorted, which makes it seem less unappealing.

BRINGING OUT THE DEAD (1999, DIR MARTIN SCORSESE)

Features a heroin subplot about a insomniac paramedic, played by Nick Cage, whose life crosses with that of a former addict, Patricia Arquette.

BLACK TAR HEROIN (1999, DIR STEVEN OKAZAKI)

Black-tar heroin (known as *chieva*) is smuggled up from Mexico and has transformed many drug scenes in Californian cities such as San Francisco. This film explores two years in the lives of five young heroin addicts – three women and two men – as they face the ever-present perils of hardcore drug addiction. One scene features 18-year-old Jessica shooting heroin into her hand and then sees her nod out and turn blue.

ANOTHER DAY IN PARADISE (1999, DIR LARRY CLARK)

James Woods and Melanie Griffith play a couple of low-lifes hooked on heroin who feed their addiction through robbery.

REQUIEM FOR A DREAM (2000, DIR DARREN ARONOFSKY)

Classic heroin movie and an adaptation of a 1978 novel by Hubert Selby Jr, this is an intelligent soul-rattling, cinematic vehicle of gruesome overindulgence. Set against the forlorn backdrop of a deteriorating Coney Island, it stars Jared Leto as Harry, a minor-league heroin dealer; his beautiful, urbane girlfriend is played by Jennifer Connelly.

JESUS' SON (2000, DIR ALISON MACLEAN)

Manic performances from loser Billy Crudup and Samantha Morton, who plot a rambling predestined course through heroin binges, petty larceny and overdose deaths. Based on a book of short stories by Denis Johnson.

TRAFFIC (2000, DIR STEVEN SODERBERGH)
A judge's daughter is sucked deeper into heroin dependency. Michael Douglas plays the judge, Benicio Del Toro a Mexican cop, and Catherine Zeta-Jones is the wife of a drugs baron.

WASTED (2002, DIR STEPHEN KAY)
Summer Phoenix, the sister of River, who died of an overdose aged 23, plays high-school girl Samantha who gets mixed up in heroin. The film is based on a true story about a plague of heroin-related deaths in a Texan town but, happily, Summer's character gets clean in the end.

HEROIN MUSIC
AN INTERVIEW WITH THE HEARTBREAKERS' JOHNNY THUNDERS
Q: What advice would you give a young musician? Would you suggest he followed the same road that you followed?

JT: I wouldn't advise anyone to follow the same road I followed. But, just read a lot, watch a lot of television and don't go out and play too much.

Q: And drugs?

JT: And drugs. And don't take drugs. It's very harmful. And that's the truth.

It's an old story. Heroin and music. Since the turn of the last century musicians have enjoyed an uneasy – and often devastating – association with heroin. It has spawned songs, even movements. Progressive rock was an unfortunate side effect of LSD; the nihilism of punk's blank generation and grunge ran on heroin. The Ramones' 'Chinese Rocks' said it all.

Musicians have been singing about it or dying from it since Charlie Parker, Miles Davis, Art Pepper, and Chet Baker defined 'cool' in the 1950s. They used heroin to ease the days between the long sweaty nights blowing their horns or mashing the piano keys. Then heroin was cool. In his frank memoir about heroin, *The Trumpet And The Spike*, Baker admits that most of the musicians he played with were on junk and that 'spiking myself became a gesture as automatic as lighting a cigarette is with you'.

> *'A connection. Remember the word, because to a junkie he is even more important than the junk itself. For if you don't have a connection – you have no junk. Junkies spend their lives waiting – waiting for the connection.'* - Chet Baker, trumpet player

The British mod scene in the early 1960s fuelled itself on purple hearts, and the hippies saw out that decade by opening their minds with LSD and magic mushrooms. Of course, heroin never really went away. Iggy Pop, Keith Richards, and Lou Reed were all users. But their influence on lifestyle didn't spread much beyond New York's East Village or those who bought The Velvet Underground's *White Light/White Heat*.

Punk's arrival in 1976 was ostensibly about blowing away anything that had gone before. Two drugs it didn't dispense with were speed and heroin. Johnny Rotten was scornful of heroin and – for the most part – the British punks at the Roxy contented themselves with amphetamine. However, heroin was prevalent on the US punk scene based around the Bowery club CBGB's and the bands that played there – Suicide, The Ramones, Richard Hell And The Voidoids, and The Heartbreakers.

Heartbreakers frontman Johnny Thunders and drummer Jerry Nolan had been on smack since using it in their former band, The New York Dolls, and their arrival on The Sex Pistols' Anarchy tour in 1976 was the cue for Sid Vicious to become dope's best punk ambassador. It was also no coincidence that The Heartbreakers' first UK single, released in 1977, was a cover of 'Chinese Rocks'. Vicious was soon a smack casualty. Out on bail on a charge of stabbing his junkie girlfriend Nancy Spungen at the Chelsea Hotel, Sid died of an accidental overdose in New York.

> *'All drug dealers got something in common, they're on a power trip. They know you're strung out and sick, they'll open the dope real*

slowly, take their time while you're sweating. They're teasing you, because they know you need them.'

- Jerry Nolan of The New York Dolls and The Heartbreakers

Cocaine and ecstasy became more common at gigs and backstage parties as the music took a turn into another decade. But heroin still had a hook on some rock stars. During much of the 1980s Mötley Crüe's Nikki Sixx fought a battle with booze and drugs during his career with the Los Angeles group. In 1987 he suffered a near-fatal heroin overdose. Boy George also fought a long battle with heroin in the early 1990s, and in 1996 Depeche Mode's Dave Gahan suffered an overdose.

However, by the early 1990s heroin wasn't playing second fiddle to any other drugs. It was *the* drug. In the USA, street heroin was becoming increasingly pure, although the price remained resolutely stable. Snorting and smoking became popular. Seattle was gaining a reputation as the heroin capital of America and one of the city's bands, Nirvana, were providing the bleak soundtrack for a new youth movement: grunge.

Grunge was all about tormented souls and melancholic chords cut with lyrics about death and drugs - preferably smack. So rock fans, who liked to play their favourite records while stoned on their favourite drug, could follow their leader. Heroin was the drug to play when they dropped the needle on *Nevermind*. Suddenly every band had a junkie, detoxing, getting busted, or passing out in photo shoots. Nirvana had Cobain. Hole had Courtney Love. Stone Temple Pilots had Scott Weiland. Alice In Chains had Layne Staley. And it didn't keep their videos off MTV. In fact it was almost a prerequisite to getting a record contract.

Staley, who was found dead at his Seattle home in 2002, penned several songs about the drug and once admitted that heroin would have 'a huge effect on my work for the rest of my life, whether I'm using or not'.

Heroin's moment had arrived. Finally. It was surprising how long it took to come out of the closet considering heroin is probably the perfect rock drug. Like the music, heroin is badass. It's Dionysian. It's romantic. It also kills. And nothing sells better in the music industry than death. It's the best career move - an instant fix for adding extra sales to a stalled album. However, it has to be the right death. Alcohol, cancer, old age are all about fading away, not burning out. But a drug overdose – preferably a heroin overdose – provides the ultimate quick burnout and immediately confers iconoclastic status: Sid, Kurt, Jimi. You don't need the surnames.

> *'Somebody called me on the phone*
> *Said hey is Dee Dee home*
> *Do you wanna take a walk*
> *Wanna go cop*
> *Wanna go get some Chinese Rock*
> *I'm livin' on Chinese Rocks*
> *All my best things are in hock*
> *I'm livin' on Chinese Rocks*
> *Everything is in the pawn shop'*
>
> – 'Chinese Rocks', The Ramones

Grunge found a fan base in Britain, but didn't produce any notable bands. Not that it mattered. Heroin was in plentiful supply. While bands like Oasis, Suede, and Elastica helped to create 'Cool Britannia', their Generation X fans were happy to adopt the drug of grunge. The smell of heroin being smoked in north London pubs during the mid-1990s became common. In a 2002 interview, Elastica's Justine Frischmann revealed the extent of heroin's grip at that time: 'Well, a lot of the people I've known who had problems with that drug [heroin], it has been about pain management,' she said. 'If people need to just…take time out from their life, it can seem better to just quietly knock yourself out and not face it or bother anyone else with it. Or kill yourself, basically.'

Opiate addiction was once so common among soldiers in Europe and the United States who had undergone battlefield surgery that it was known as 'the soldiers' disease'. They spent years on a legal supply of the drug – and it did them no damage.

And that's the other part of heroin's attraction to musicians. It might not have the mind altering properties of acid, but it can still remove the user from the real world. And that's useful on tour. Who wants to be up all the while? Or down? Heroin can smooth the transition between the highs of a show and the 1,000 miles of slow road between boredom and nowhere. Musicians have also admitted that a fix can be good for performances because, like alcohol, it relaxes – although, unlike alcohol, it doesn't significantly affect coordination and means that the guitarist is not going to mess up a chord sequence.

SONGS ABOUT HEROIN

ARTIST	SONG TITLES
The Velvet Underground	'Waiting For The Man', 'Heroin'
Alice In Chains	'Junkhead', 'God Smack'
The Cure	'Heroin Face', 'Coming Up'
The Rolling Stones	'Brown Sugar', 'Sister Morphine'
The Stranglers	'Golden Brown'
Iggy Pop	'My Girl Hates My Heroin', 'Heroin Makes You'
The Only Ones	'The Beast', 'It's The Truth'
Neil Young	'The Needle And The Damage Done'
Guns N'Roses	'Mr Brownstone'
My Dying Bride	'Heroin Chic'
Everclear	'Heroin Girl'
The Ramones	'Chinese Rocks'
The Lurkers	'Heroin It's All Over'
Johnny Thunders	'Too Much Junkie Business'
The Cherubs	'Heroin Man'
No Man	'Housewives Hooked On Heroin'
The Wildhearts	'Heroin'
James Brown	'King Heroin'
Lou Reed	'The Last Shot'
Bert Jansch	'Needle Of Death'
Counting Crows	'Mr Jones'
Elliot Smith	'Needle In The Hay'
Pink Floyd	'Comfortably Numb'
Nirvana	'Something In The Way'

Once off the tour bus, heroin's use doesn't end. After a long and gruelling series of concerts, what better way of blocking out the anxiety and stress of having to face up to the world without the support of management and lackeys, and the camaraderie of group and crew?

In an age of soundbites and image, heroin is also a short-cut to providing much-needed credibility for a band. A band's well-publicized narcotic leanings give them a dangerous allure, and journalists only have to mention the guitarist's problems with fixing up and the piece will immediately have the frisson of danger that sells magazines. They will probably also be mentioned in the same breath as Kurt Cobain, which can't hurt. Heroin is no longer career suicide.

> '**When I'm closing in on death**
> **Heroin be the death of me**
> **When I'm rushing on my run**
> **And I feel just like Jesus' son'**
> 'Heroin', Lou Reed

It also became relatively available and, with purity levels rising, music fans could keep up a habit to match those of their idols. The weekend rocker didn't have to worry about his track marks being uncovered by the boss at his law practice – the increased purity of the drug meant that snorting was possible and the biggest obstacle to the first-time user, the needle, was no longer necessary.

Ultimately, however, heroin became the fashionable drug of choice for musicians and fans in the 1990s because it upped the ante on the cocaine-snorting, speed-gobbling, acid-flashing youth movements of previous generations. Rebellion is the voice of youth and every new generation wants its own identity. It also wants to scare authority more than the last movement. So where acid house had smiley T-shirts, light-sticks and ecstasy, the fashion accessories of grunge were plaid, tattoos and heroin.

> '**I am not a preacher but drugs killed a lot of great men'** 'Needle And The Damage Done', Neil Young

Heroin also suited the times and subculture that developed around grunge and the message its bands were selling: Life Sucks; I'm A Loser. This was the sound of hopelessness. The rage of despair. It had an immediate resonance with its audience of slackers. This wasn't a political message, it was nihilistic. Suburban college kids who saw their future stretching out in front of them in a succession of McJobs could identify with these wounded, strung-out heroes. Heroin came along to take their pain away.

HEROIN-RELATED DEATHS IN ROCK

- In 1959 Billie Holiday finally succumbed to the twin ravages of heart disease and heroin under police arrest on a hospital bed.
- Frankie Lymon's career came to an abrupt stop in 1968 when the singing sensation (he was the frontman in Frankie Lymon And The Teenagers) was discovered on the bathroom floor of a New York apartment with a syringe by his side.
- In 1970 the hit of the Monterey Pop Festival, Janis Joplin died of an accidental heroin overdose in the bedroom of her suite at the Hollywood Landmark Hotel. At 27, she was at the peak of her short career.
- Jimi Hendrix died of a barbiturate overdose within weeks of Joplin, but the 27-year-old guitarist had been a known user of heroin.
- Aged 27, Jim Morrison was found dead of heart failure in the bath at his Paris apartment in 1971. The full facts surrounding the premature death of The Doors' vocalist in the early hours of the morning are still unclear, although it is thought he acquired a fix earlier that night and, if that didn't cause the fatal heart attack, many blame his death on the cumulative effects of his heavy drug use.
- The 24-year-old Scottish drummer of The Average White Band, Robbie McIntosh, was killed at a Hollywood party in 1974 after he was spiked with a lethal dose of heroin.
- Tim Buckley died in his sleep in 1975 after snorting prodigious amounts of heroin supplied by a friend.
- Just months after his girlfriend Nancy Spungen was found stabbed to death in New York's Chelsea Hotel, punk rocker Sid Vicious scored a lethal dose of heroin and suffered a fatal overdose in his sleep. He was 21.
- Darby Crash of the Los Angeles punk band The Germs died of an overdose at the end of 1980, just a week after reforming the group.

- After years of heroin addiction and a career that remained resolutely underrated, singer/songwriter Tim Hardin died at the end 1980.
- Malcolm Owen of UK punk group The Ruts, who dealt with his heroin addiction in many of the band's lyrics, lost his battle with the drug in 1980.
- Heroin split The Pretenders, literally. Guitarist James Honeyman-Scott and bass player Pete Farndon both met their ends after taking speedballs in 1982 and 1983 respectively.
- Red Hot Chili Peppers lost their 26-year-old lead guitarist when Hillel Slovak's drug lifestyle caught up with him and he died of an overdose in 1988.
- Chet Baker was hooked most of his adult life. Before his death in 1988 - falling from a hotel room in Amsterdam - the drug ravaged his film-idol looks, drew him beatings from connections, earned him dozens of busts on narcotic violations, and landed him a spell in Riker's Island jail.
- After more than a decade of heavy drug abuse, the former New York Dolls and Heartbreakers guitarist Johnny Thunders died of heroin overdose in New Orleans in 1991. The proto-punk, who was 38 at the time of his death, recorded The Ramones' classic 'Chinese Rocks' and often played it at gigs.
- In 1994, Nirvana's Kurt Cobain was found dead. The guitarist/vocalist with the Seattle-based grunge band, had struggled with years of smack abuse. Although Cobain shot himself, he delivered the self-inflicted fatal injury just a week after almost succumbing to a heroin overdose.
- Kristen Pfaff, the 27-year-old bassist in Courtney Love's female grunge band Hole, died of an overdose in a bathroom in 1994.
- The drug-related lifestyle of Grateful Dead's Jerry Garcia finally caught up with him in 1995 when he died from health complications during withdrawal from heroin addiction.
- While preparing for a Blind Melon concert in New Orleans in 1995, the group's 23-year-old singer, Shannon Hoon, died of an overdose.
- Jonathan Melvoin, a keyboardist with Smashing Pumpkins, died of an overdose in a Manhattan hotel in 1996.

■ In 2002, Alice In Chains' lead singer Layne Staley was found dead in his Seattle home. Staley's long-time battle with drug dependency was a central component of the band's sound, which included the song 'Junkhead'.

HEROIN LITERATURE

Books about smack are a writer's dream. All that hollow-cheeked desperation and grubby hopelessness sends authors scurrying to their word processors, clutching their thesauruses tightly. Junkie lit offers opportunities for some unremittingly bleak prose, dark, dark characters – everyone loves a loser and you can't get a better loser than a junkie – and a dramatic final chapter in which someone overdoses in a grubby council flat.

The appeal of heroin is, of course, its illegality and the glamour that goes with being on the wrong side of the law. Characters on the margins of society are manna from heaven to an author who doesn't want to litter his pages with boring Mr and Mrs Normals who go to work, drive to the supermarket, and enjoy a schooner of sherry at the weekend.

As a plot device, heroin can take off in any direction the author wants to go – from introspective angst, as in Alexander Trocchi's *Cain's Book*, to crazy road odyssey in *Go Now* by Richard Hell. The rituals connected with heroin use, from the cooking to the injecting, are excellent vehicles to show off literary dexterity. The vocabulary for jacking up can easily up a writer's word count if the plot is running out of steam, and those similes and adjectives just can't be reined in when it comes to writing about veins, needles, and blood.

'Dope was so magic. We were Romeo and Juliet. It was just what I'd always wanted without even knowing it, stuff that lets you not only dream while awake, but gives you the power to prod and stroke and sculpt the dreams... With junk you can dream your life.' Richard Hell in his novel *Go Now*

Beyond the physical, heroin can take on deeper complexities, and address the issues of hedonism, nihilism and existentialism – all the big ideas that authors who want to be

Computer graphic of a molecule of heroin (diacetylmorphine, or diamorphine). Heroin was first synthesized from morphine in 1898 and is used in some countries to relieve severe pain.

Equipment used to prepare and inject heroin, the white powder shown here, which is usually sold in silver foil. To prepare it for injection, the powder is mixed with water and dissolved in a heated spoon. The solution is then injected into a vein using the needle and syringe.

taken seriously like to bandy about in their books. There are moral ambiguities inherent in novels about heroin and, for the reader who prefers a happy ending, there's always the epilogue option in which the user is redeemed through the love of a good woman (or man) and signs up to a methadone programme.

THOMAS DE QUINCEY

There's no doubt that heroin has inspired a wealth of ground-breaking and searing work, all the more so when written by an author with first-hand experience of addiction. This applies to one of the earliest memoirs on the subject – Thomas De Quincey's *Confessions Of An English Opium Eater*, published in 1822.

This autobiographical account of his opium addiction is De Quincey's most famous work. The writer took opium to ease physical pain but became addicted to it. The book charts the psychological effects of the drug – from the euphoria of his initial experiences to the darkness and nightmares arising from long-term usage. Richly written, it is a seminal tale of the effects of addiction on a brilliant mind.

COLLINS, KIPLING, AND CROWLEY

In the days when books about drug addiction were frowned upon, it was a very daring author who would break the taboo and shine a light on such behaviour. In Wilkie Collins' 1868 novel *The Moonstone*, opium is used as a plot device for both its medicinal properties and its exotic and deviant connotations. Franklin Blake steals the diamond against his own knowledge after he has secretly been given a nightcap laced with laudanum. Collins' ambivalent attitude towards the drug can be explained by his own addiction to the substance.

Rudyard Kipling's 1901 novel *Kim* also makes a pointed comment about the ready availability of opium in India, and its power to addict and corrupt. In the book, Kim's father 'came across the woman who smoked opium and learned the taste from her, and died as poor whites died in India'.

In 1922 Aleister Crowley shocked British Victorian society with his book *Diary Of A Drug Fiend*. Crowley called himself Beast 666, totally rejected the Victorian hypocrisy of his day and was a constant user of heroin, cocaine, opium, hash, and peyote. *Diary Of A Drug Fiend* was an eye-opener to those who knew little of drugs, but Crowley wanted to show the true nature of drug addiction, that there were moments of joy and elation, not just despair.

It's the story of a young man and woman who fall madly in love and whirl through Europe in a frenzied heroin and cocaine adventure. Their joyful existence is brought to an end when their supply is cut off and they are forced to reappraise their existence with the help of the mysterious King Lamus.

Crowley's personal experiences ran like a river through the book, which certainly gave Middle England a shudder. Some 30 years later, in the USA, William S Burroughs caused a similar furore when his book *Junky* came out in 1953. Today heroin is everywhere – from housing estates to public-school common rooms – but when Crowley and Burroughs were writing, coming clean about addiction and writing books about it were not in an author's job description. In fact, the first edition of *Junky* was published under the pseudonym William Lee.

WILLIAM S BURROUGHS

Burroughs is the classic junkie lit author who lived it, and *Junky* is generally regarded as a classic of its type. Junky starkly recounts Burroughs' decades-long addiction to heroin. Written when the USA was in the grip of anti-drug hysteria, the first edition contained a number of disclaimers by the publisher whenever Burroughs made some unorthodox claims about the nature of addiction. The disclaimers were outlined at the beginning: 'For the protection of the reader, we have inserted occasional parenthetical notes to indicate where the author clearly departs from accepted medical fact or makes unsubstantiated statements in an effort to justify his actions.'

Burroughs always maintained that heroin addiction never damaged him physically or hindered the creative process of his writing. He would cite De Quincey's relatively long life (he died at 72 despite suffering from tuberculosis) as proof that one could survive heroin relatively unscathed (Burroughs himself survived until he was 83). His experiences as an addict coloured much of his work and he argued that without heroin he wouldn't have become the author he was, and that his most successful work, 1959's *Naked Lunch*, wouldn't have been written.

ALEXANDER TROCCHI

Yet there are others who believe the contrary, that heroin destroys brains and creativity. In 1960, *Cain's Book* by cult Scottish writer Alexander Trocchi was published. Known as the 'Scottish Beat', Trocchi was a heroin addict who turned his young wife to prostitution to pay for drugs.

Considered to be his finest work, *Cain's Book* is the semi-autobiographical tale of a heroin addict writer who finds he can't write. Norman Mailer said at the time 'It is different from other books, it is true, it has art, it is brave.' It was the last book Trocchi wrote (he died in 1984) and John Calder, who published Trocchi's books in the UK believes heroin destroyed the writer and deprived the world of a significant literary talent.

JIM CARROLL

In 1978 the role of author who lived it was passed on to the poet, playwright, musician and author Jim Carroll whose memoirs, *The Basketball Diaries*, were based on his own heroin addiction. The book covers the period 1962–6 when the teenage Carroll growing up on the mean streets of New York. He tells of his posh private schooling and his years playing basketball, stealing and hustling gay men to support his growing heroin addiction. It's a powerful, first-hand account of heroin addiction without any lapses into moral judgement. There's no 'Just Say No' admonitions, no cloying self-pity. Carroll has the grace to allow his readers to come to their own conclusions.

In the 1980s heroin seemed to have been overtaken by other drugs as a literary muse. Writers like Brett Easton Ellis and Jay McInerney favoured cocaine and tranquillizers as plot drivers, and bright young things snorting Charlie from toilet seats occupied young fashionable novelists. Heroin all but disappeared from the bookshelves and it wasn't until the 1990s that it made a comeback – in spectacular fashion.

Grunge music and the aura surrounding heroin chic put smack right back on top of the bestseller lists. The plethora of cheap heroin meant that more people were using, which meant more material for budding novelists, and the availability of heroin was such that addicts were just as likely to come from a bleak Detroit housing project, as a three-storey London townhouse. Anyone could score. The perfect conditions for a resurgence of junkie lit.

Heroin also allows rich kids to dabble in the underworld and suffer like they've never suffered before. It brings them to the brink and they can write about squalor and dirty needles along with complex ideas that they may have picked up in their creative writing classes.

It's no surprise, then, that much of the heroin literature churned out in the late 1980s and 1990s – all slick covers and tough talk – have used heroin as the central character, and relegated the flesh-and-blood components to the supporting cast. And for every riveting description of jacking up, there's a tedious, turgid wodge of text breaking down the process to its dull, everyday components. The protagonists of books like Linda Yablonsky's semi-autobiographical novel *The Story Of Junk* and Peter Trachtenberg's memoir *7 Tattoos* are swamped by the mechanics of drug use, which the authors clearly find more fascinating than characterization and plot.

> 'Heroin was a way of being vulnerable, as a girl was supposed to be, and yet daring, as she wasn't.' From *How To Stop Time: Heroin From A To Z* by Ann Marlowe

Part of the problem is that the user-turned-writer is perhaps not best placed to bring the subject alive and it's a fine line between writing a visceral, gritty account of addiction and a matter-of-fact trawl through drug dependency. In *Naked Lunch*, William Burroughs writes, 'Remembering a period of heavy addiction is like playing back a tape recording of events experienced by the front brain alone. Flat statements of external events. "I went to the store and bought some brown sugar. I came home and ate half the box. I took a three grain shot." Complete absence of nostalgia in these memories.' Perhaps that explains why books that are just about heroin can be so flat and characterless.

Heroin can just be so bleak. And, without the help of characters and plot, can bludgeon the non-using reader. Ann Marlowe's 1999 book *How To Stop Time: Heroin From A To Z* is an alphabetic trawl through heroin and heroin addiction written in a no-nonsense style. Marlowe uses her personal experience of the drug to weave an entertaining journal of analysis and homespun philosophy about the drug. But, by the end, the total immersion in heroin leaves the reader gasping for air and desperate for another layer of intrigue besides the art of scoring smack or getting to sleep at night.

It probably took the work of Will Self in the 1990s and Irvine Welsh's *Trainspotting* to revitalize the genre. Self, journalist and writer, first injected heroin at 17 and was a full-time junkie for almost 20 years. Many of his short stories and articles deal with heroin and addiction, but he is strongest when writing about the drug as an incidental element within a story.

In *How The Dead Live*, a dead woman watches over her living daughters, one of them being the heroin-addicted Natasha. Natasha's addiction may be a thinly veiled portrait of his own experience, but that's neither here nor there. The novel's themes of contemporary life and the search for meaning are what interests the reader.

Welsh could never be accused of taking his subject too seriously and although he doesn't stint on the despair of addiction, he manages to wring a lot of humour from his subject. The protagonists have no future, but Welsh doesn't moralize. There's no hint of I-told-you-so and the pages are alive with the sheer pleasure of taking heroin. After all, when life doesn't hold much else, you might as well get pleasure from somewhere.

The appeal of heroin to this latest generation of writers goes beyond its illegal status. Heroin doesn't give up. It has a definite hold on a writer like no other drug – especially a writer who is an ex-user. Luke Davies is a poet and writer whose novel *Candy* didn't follow the usual drug novel path. It's a love story first and a heroin novel second and, although the presence of heroin is powerful and all-pervading, the relationship between two people and the nature of obsession is the central theme.

Similarly, Ellen Miller's debut novel, *Like Being Killed*, is the story of a brilliant, caustic, masochistic Jewish junkie named Ilyana Meyerovich and her fraught relationship with her wholesome, maternal room-mate,

Susie. It's because Miller has devoted time to creating her characters rather than just making them play second fiddle to junk that the story is so powerful. Miller has said that the friendship between the two women already contained 'the seeds of its own destruction' and the book would have only elicited 'So what?' comments if it had simply been about drugs. And then more drugs.

HEROIN FICTION AND MEMOIRS

GO ASK ALICE (ANONYMOUS, ARROW)

The shocking, real-life diary of a young adolescent girl facing the world alone. And then facing it with drugs. Sad, hopeful, moving, despairing, inevitably tragic, Go Ask Alice is a testament to the dangers of growing up in a unforgiving world today.

PERMANENT MIDNIGHT (JERRY STAHL, ABACUS)

TV writer Jerry Stahl recounts how he slipped into an opiated abyss and then clawed his way out. Beneath Stahl's successful front as a scriptwriter ran a toxic undercurrent of madness, hard narcotics and hardcore sex. In 1998, it was turned into a major feature film starring Ben Stiller.

JUNK (MELVIN BURGESS, PUFFIN BOOKS)

Tar and Gemma are the two teenage runaways in love who end up on the streets and in the grip of smack. The prose is unflinching as the story charts the lovers' harrowing downhill spiral from their first blissful hit to their inevitable grubby decline. A love story between boy, girl and needle. Aimed at teenagers, Junk caused a furore on publication – graphic descriptions of drug abuse and the all-pervading sense of youthful despair set the moral majority in a spin. Enid Blyton it ain't.

THE LOTUS CREW (STEWART MEYER, SERPENT'S TAIL)

Set in New York's seedy Lower East Side, The Lotus Crew tells the story of a gangster's son Tommy and his junkie partner Alvira. The tough-talking twosome carve out a lucrative drug-dealing operation and are respected in the underworld for 'putting out the best bag in New York'. Things turn sour when they couple are betrayed by one of their own and are forced to exact a bloody revenge.

CAIN'S BOOK (ALEXANDER TROCCHI, CALDER PUBLICATIONS)
An honest account of the highs and lows of heroin addiction by someone who experienced it at first hand. At times disturbing, often moving, the book is searingly honest about the day-to-day tedium of trying to score and maintain some kind of equilibrium. The subject matter isn't one to incite cheer, but Trocchi manages to lift the story from the depths of human misery to create something almost magical. A neglected masterpiece.

CONFESSIONS OF AN ENGLISH OPIUM EATER
(THOMAS DE QUINCEY, PENGUIN BOOKS)
The gripping tale of the author's early life as an opium addict at a time when the drug was as easy to get hold of as a new handkerchief. De Quincey, despite his many talents and ready charm, was something of an outsider and opium gave him confidence. This is the story of his terrifying mental and physical torments as an addict. He recounts, with unrelenting clarity, the wild swings between ecstasy and despair. It's a stark illustration of the part played by opium in the degeneration of a flawed but brilliant mind.

TRAINSPOTTING (IRVINE WELSH, MINERVA)
The book that managed to make junk funny without stinting on the harsh realities of drug abuse. Set in the underbelly of Edinburgh, it features a gang of lads locked into a cycle of getting high, getting laid and getting high. The humour is caustic. The filth is real. And the world of addiction – and the descent from purity to heroin hell – is horrifying.

WILL O'THE WISP
(PIERRE DRIEU LA ROCHELLE, MARION BOYARS PUBLISHERS)
A minor smack classic, which charts the destruction of a man who becomes hooked on heroin.

REQUIEM FOR A DREAM
(HUBERT SELBY JR, MARION BOYARS PUBLISHERS)

The moral of this book is 'Don't sample the merchandise.' Written in Selby's grim tell-it-like-it-is prose, it's the story of two friends desperate to make good. They work hard, stay sober and buy a substantial haul of Class A drugs. They are successful dealers and the American Dream is within their grasp until they spoil it all by trying out the gear for themselves. After that, it's downhill all the way.

LIKE BEING KILLED (ELLEN MILLER, VIRAGO)

Ilyana Meyerovich is a self-confessed suicidal strung-out Jew. Her new flatmate, Susie Lyons, is her complete opposite – a blonde, naïve, artistic and optimistic woman. Like Being Killed takes the sisterhood theme to the edge as the two needy women dramatically connect and begin their downward spiral, helped along by copious amounts of heroin. The consequences are disastrous.

DIARY OF A DRUG FIEND (ALEISTER CROWLEY, WEISER BOOKS)

Crowley's first published novel and another drug classic, Diary Of A Drug Fiend presented a shocking interpretation of heroin and cocaine addiction to a society unfamiliar with widespread drug use. Crowley – himself a constant user of heroin, cocaine, opium, hashish, and peyote – drew on his deep personal experiences to tell the story of a young man and woman who fall in love and set off on a heroin/cocaine-fuelled journey through Europe. Their unbridled joy in each other and their drugs is abruptly scuppered when their narcotics supply is cut off. But, before despair threatens to overwhelm them both, the couple are taken under the wing of King Lamus, who helps them to free themselves from the hellishness of addiction through magic. Throughout the novel, Crowley makes a point of explaining the realities of drug use and emphasizes that heroin users are capable of intelligent thought and reason despite their dependency on the drug.

THE STORY OF JUNK (LINDA YABLONSKY, REVIEW)

The setting of this film is yuppie New York during the early 1980s.

The story revolves around two female heroin users who are set up for a bust. The plot is driven by their quest to find out who set them up and why.

7 TATTOOS (PETER TRACHTENBERG, CROWN PUBLISHING)

Trachtenberg's memoir of a life lived on the edge in unsavoury, seamy detail. The book is a frank trawl through the grubby underworld and brings to light the introspective suffering and doubt that plagues drug users and non-drug users alike.

GO NOW: A NOVEL (RICHARD HELL, FOURTH ESTATE)

Punk rock survivor Richard Hell turns novelist with the story of Billy, a burnt-out drug- and sex-addicted punk. Billy hooks up with a former girlfriend, Chrissa, and the pair embark on a cataclysmic cross-country writing assignment with a stash of junk to help them through the trip. A former smack addict himself, the former guitarist with US bands Television, The Heartbreakers and The Voidoids creates a highly personal interpretation of dependency, and grittily recreates the inner workings of an addict's mind.

HOW TO STOP TIME: HEROIN FROM A TO Z (ANN MARLOWE, VIRAGO)

Literally an alphabetic – from abstention to youth, via habit and narcosis – trawl through heroin and heroin addiction written in a no-nonsense style. No glamour and no moralizing. Marlowe uses her personal experience of the drug (she was a user for seven years) to weave analysis and philosophy about the drug. Heroin, just the way it is.

JUNKY (WILLIAM BURROUGHS, PENGUIN BOOKS)

The benchmark for all smack literature, Burroughs' first novel is a warts-and-all depiction of the addict's life. It's all here – hallucinations, desperation, hunger for the needle. Set around a sordid 1940s underground in which the inhabitants care only for opium, morphine, heroin, dilaudid, pantopan, codeine, and dionine. The prose is frank and sometimes shocking in its casual acknowledgement of junk as part of everyday life.

CANDY: A NOVEL OF LOVE AND ADDICTION
(LUKE DAVIES, BALLENTINE BOOKS)
This is a novel about heroin addiction from the heady narcissism of the narrator's first forays with his new love, Candy, and the relative innocence of their shared addiction, this novel charts their moral decline. It is painful, tender.

FIRST PERSON
MIKE HALL, MUSICIAN AND FORMER HEROIN ADDICT
'I had a friend called Jenny. She often came to stay with me and I used to lecture her and say she was crazy and shouldn't do it [heroin]. I guess I was about 17 then, living in Archway in north London. From very early on virtually all my friends were older than me. I'm a drummer and I'd played the Marquee Club when I was about 13 so I was often surrounded and influenced by people a lot older than me.

'I don't know what the motivation was, but Jenny got really pissed off with me lecturing her about her using heroin and one day I went over to her place just to pick up some dope to smoke and she gave me about £10 [$15] of heroin. I took it purely out of curiosity even though I knew it was stupid. I snorted it. And it was just overwhelmingly beautiful. Some people who take it for the first time get really sick; I know people get all sorts of different reactions. But I took it and found it completely amazing.

> 'People who take heroin aren't necessarily evil people. But they may do evil things as a result of what it forces you to do.' Mike Hall

'It just made me feel completely at ease, absolutely comfortable and euphoric. So for about a year and a half I thought "This is great." But I also thought there would be no way I would end up taking it all the while. I just took it about every three weeks, snorting it. I got into taking heroin not out of trauma or depression, but curiosity. That is a scary thing, because I was quite level headed. Even so the curiosity got me in. It's a gorgeous, gorgeous feeling. Then just slipping into it.

'For people who want to bury something heroin is a very good temporary option. But I wasn't depressed at the time. I was just enjoying it. It's not something I'd describe as true happiness, but in a superficial way I felt that I was quite happy. Everything was really exciting. There was a lot of music stuff going on. You'd do a gig, go to a party. And then Johnny Thunders [former guitarist with The New York Dolls and The Heartbreakers] came to London to do some gigs. This was around 1982 and I did a session with Thunders, who was heavily into dope. The heroin thing was just around and if you're in an environment like that

'There is no drug known to man that becomes safer when its production and distribution are handed over to criminals.' Professor Norman Zinberg, Harvard Medical School

you lose sight of the objections to it – in a strange way, this becomes the norm. It no longer seems something very scary because it is always there. Also, if you're dropping LSD night and day then you're not going to be much use to anybody. But with heroin it just affects your central nervous system. You can do what you normally do. Thunders envied me because he had been taking smack for so many years he could never get that stoned.

'At this time I was taking heroin occasionally, about once every three weeks. But then it became once a week, then two or three days running and I'd think, "Whoa this has got to stop." I can't say exactly when I thought I actually needed to get some help, although I was only 18. The ability to stop after the third day, when I thought it would be sensible, became less and less. I couldn't stop.

'The insidious thing is that it would normally scare an intelligent person, but it kind of doesn't because heroin numbs you so well. It numbs your whole experience of life. So you don't hear those alarm bells going off. You start off with all your faculties together. You think, "This is really stupid thing to get into it." But the more you take the less the antennae are up to warn you. The overriding desire to have that comfort, that ability to escape becomes greater than anything else.

'Absolutely, I thought I could handle it. I never, ever, thought I'd be silly enough to get hooked. I thought I'd be in control. There were people I knew who on the surface seemed to be doing that. But it only takes a small period in your life when you kind of let go and then you get to a point where you physically feel ill without it.

'What I remember most is probably the first year and a half I took heroin, I really enjoyed it. I really enjoyed the effect and the lifestyle. It was a constant party, not having to face any feelings, not having to confront anything. That maybe lasted for a year and a half and I was having a great time.

'I had a period where I injected heroin and cocaine, and it was a phenomenal high and many times I'd do that and feel my heart go boom, boom, boom. How I'm not dead from that I don't know. Maybe I'm very lucky but I obviously was protected somehow. The heroin numbs you to things like that so it never worried me. I was quite careful though. Most overdoses I heard about were about people who'd stopped and then come back to it because their tolerance level had dropped.

'I started off injecting £10 [$15] worth, which would be about an eighth of a gram and the most I probably injected was a quarter of a gram, which was quite a lot. I was careful in some ways and then I wasn't careful. I was careful with heroin, but not cocaine. I did loads of coke.

'The remaining four years I was taking heroin was a nightmare on the whole. I wished with everything I had that I didn't have to take this stuff. I went from snorting it to smoking it and from smoking it I really damaged my lungs. They are still sensitive now and this is after 16 years of being heroin free and 10 years of not smoking anything at all. They are still quite bad but infinitely better than they were. It got to a point when I was about 19 when I just couldn't breathe at all. I almost died through an asthma attack and just managed to drive myself in time to St Thomas's Hospital in London to go on a ventilator. It scars your lungs to bits. You've got all the fumes from the foil, intense heat from the heroin; it just burns your lungs away. As a result of this scarring I injected heroin for the last couple of years of taking it, between 1984-6. I always got someone to do it for me because I hated doing it. I hate needles. I was a hopeless injecting addict.

'Of course, I tried getting off it. I didn't try to stop without anything. Once or twice – and I was lucky it was only once or twice – I couldn't get any drugs and it was horrible, just horrible. The most uncomfortable feeling. I felt really cold, shivery, every muscle was aching. I remember lying in a bed in Clapham and it would be maybe lunchtime before I had any hope of getting any heroin. I would just lie there feeling absolutely terrified about...these feelings. And they were getting worse and worse. This just reinforced my terror of the thought of giving up.

'The only way I can explain it is if you liken it to smoking cigarettes. If you smoke addictively (and I certainly used to) I think you have a little bit of fear about not being able to smoke. If you're in a cinema after about two hours you would give anything to have a cigarette. Heroin, to me was about ten times worse. It's like if you are in a desert or something and desperate to have a glass of water. Every cell in your body, every single part of your being, is craving for that thing. Then you have heroin and there is an amazing sense of relief.

'I started to get methadone in the last four years because I didn't like being addicted to heroin. A private doctor in Kilburn prescribed methadone for me. This was near a 24-hour chemist in Kilburn. You could buy syringes there. On my first appointment I had to take methadone and then go back an hour or so later so the doctor could observe me. If you didn't really have an addiction you would be stoned, but I wasn't.

Research conducted by the UK Home Office in 1998 found that over 70 per cent of those using drugs were financing their habits through shoplifting, about 30 per cent through dealing and just over 10 per cent through legitimate work.

'The idea was to use the methadone and then use it less and less. But I ended up using both. Heroin is so much about tolerance. I was taking anything up to £200 [$290] a day at the end and I wasn't particularly stoned. That's partly how I got into dealing. I fell into that. I had previously sold cannabis to make some money but it was not sufficient to fund my ever-increasing habit. The friend I went to, where I was getting my dope, had much better stuff than anyone else. So in a naive way I thought I was doing a service for everyone because they were getting ripped off everywhere else. So my friend says, "Instead of keep coming around why don't I just give you three and a half grams and then you give me the money when you've got it." So that's how I fell into it. You can't excuse it.

'This was around the summer of 1982. I was living in Battersea Park Road at the time and later moved to Notting Hill dealing little bits of drugs, but that wasn't making enough money. I never sold to people who had never done heroin before. I really wouldn't. I would also get people bits of methadone to help them to stop. I just thought it was a terrible thing to be getting into. The people I was selling to were people who were getting it everyday anyway and they were getting it cheaper. Of course, what happened then was if you've got a huge bag of heroin lying about, you

In the past 10 years Singapore has executed at least 100 drug traffickers for possession of small amounts of heroin, according to Amnesty International.

start using silly amounts and you can afford to use that because it's the profits you are doing. It's much cheaper when you buy it wholesale.

'In 1984 I went to rehab in Tooting when my drug taking was at its worst. I did get off heroin and moved to Cardiff for four months to work for a friend, but every three weeks I came back to London. I had really wanted to give up but lacked the determination and control not to slip back. I didn't have the right thought processes and I moved back to London at Christmas and got straight back into it.

'Later, in the summer of 1986 – as a result of being friends with a couple of girls that knew and supplied Boy George – I was tricked into selling some heroin to a journalist from the *Sunday People*. He knew someone I knew and said, "So and so says you don't normally do this, but is it all right?" Knowing how horrible it can be to be sick from withdrawal symptoms, I agreed. Next thing, one Saturday night, I woke up at 10pm near King's Cross. I had a flat in Highbury at the time and before I went home I popped down to King's Cross to pick up the Sunday papers to see what was in them. I get to the news stand and there's this headline: "Lock Up This Man Now". Next to it was a picture of me.

'The report said I was supplying drugs to Boy George, which wasn't true. But they had a name and a picture and fabricated story. I read the paper standing outside the station and thought, "Fuck it." I knew that in the morning it was going be everywhere and I had to get out of London. You never see these things at the time, but in retrospect it was probably one of the best things that happened to me.

'So I went to my brother's flat because I had my methadone stashed there. I wanted to get my methadone and get out of London before I was caught. I drove through the night to Cornwall because I thought I could stay with my mum, but my stepdad wouldn't let me as they were so traumatized by seeing the newspaper. They had a hotel down there at the time and all the papers – with me on the front – had arrived for the guests to read.

'I felt almost suicidal then and had nowhere to go. I decided to drive to Wales. I'd been driving all night so I was pretty tired. I drove to my cousin's place. Adrian was pretty cool and wanted to help me. He put me in touch with a friend, Phil, who knew of a great solicitor and we decided to contact the police, who were after me because of the slanderous newspaper report.

'The local police in South Wales came around to Phil's house and took me to a tiny police station for questioning. Then the police from Paddington Green in London came down to take me back on the train. I remember one of the policemen was pretty good and said, "All I want to do is to get you off heroin." That was pretty amazing, I thought at the time, for a policeman, and he genuinely meant it and, ultimately, I think I was saved when I was arrested. I had no choice. I had a very strong habit when I was arrested and I knew whichever way I went I would have to stop taking heroin. If I wanted to have half a chance of not being sent to prison and doing probation or something like that, I knew I would have to stop taking heroin. I probably needed that ultimatum.

'I was charged with supplying heroin to persons unknown, which at that time could have drawn between five to seven years. They also charged me with possession because they found bits of heroin in my car. So it was pretty heavy. But I was fortunate.

'I went to the Whitchurch Hospital in Cardiff, which specialized in alcohol and drugs, and was put on a drastic reducing programme of methadone. I was there two and a half weeks, which should have started out at about 60ml of methadone and gradually reduced. But the doctors knew about the seriousness of my court case and I was started off with a low amount and I was really ill, just desperately uncomfortable and waking with cold sweats. It's like having a jackhammer going off in your head. The withdrawal from heroin is a few days, the withdrawal from methadone is much longer and I was addicted to both. I think what stops most heroin addicts from giving up is the sheer terror of the withdrawal. I'd warn anyone against taking methadone for a long time. I did about ten days without sleeping, which just does your head in, and ended up being asked to leave because I was caught smoking dope to help me sleep.

'So I moved to Cornwall and found myself waking up in terrible nightmares, terrible sweating. I couldn't sleep and I'd get up and have walks by the sea. I didn't have any money, which was a blessing because if I had for the first ten months I would have gone straight back. I didn't have any friends in Cornwall so I had a lot of really weak moments in those months. Fortunately, the temptation was overridden by the sheer inconvenience of it all. I was 300 miles [480km] from London and there wasn't any heroin around in Cornwall then that I knew about. Also, I knew consciously it would be a disaster to take it again, but only slowly did the physical thing abate. My probation officer travelled 300 miles [480km] to the court to help me out and I walked out of the court with two years' probation, to run concurrently. This was largely because I had been drug free for four months, had taken a job in my mother's hotel and had started to rebuild my life.

'For years I was scared of the memory of it. I was so scared. Every time I came to London I would have shivers down my spine. Or if I saw one of the places I used to go I would just…just the memory. If it doesn't physically kill you, it kills your spirit. You are so numb to it. It's the ultimate numbing chemical.

'Up until the time I got on to drugs I was massively overweight, but I lost lots of weight taking drugs. Then when I gave up heroin I put it all on again and more. I went to about 18 stone [114kg] and I remember walking up a hill in Cornwall and it just clicked. I was 23. Something clicked. I thought, 'I've given up heroin, something that is supposed to be the hardest thing in the world to give up, and now I can't get up this fucking hill." I was sweating, my lungs were shot. I decided to get fit and lost about five stones [32kg] and never went back to being fat.

'But my health has suffered from all this. My lungs from smoking heroin. But the cruellest part is that I also picked up hepatitis C and didn't know anything about it until 1999. This was a massive shock as I had been free from heroin for 13 years and had been extremely healthy for at least ten of those years. Soon after I gave up in 1988 I got into a depression for about a year and a half when I thought wanted to die. I started to practise the Buddhism of Nichiren Daishonin in 1990 and overcame my depression remarkably. I gave up smoking cigarettes even, and began to feel completely alive and very happy – more happy than ever before in my life. The practice, and its philosophy, has helped to heal me beyond recognition and has enabled me to live life fully and realise many dreams. I learnt from all my mistakes and began to and still have a great career with music.

> 'I used to have to wear sunglasses because my eyes were so used to being pinpricks. I ended up wearing sunglasses for three months.' Mike Hall

'However, in 1999 I started to feel like I was poisoned, I was very tired and always got colds. I went to my doctor who thought I was stressed out, but I knew it was more than that. Three days before the millennium they told me I had got hepatitis C. This was heroin creeping back at me – the absolute strictness of cause and effect. By then I was so much a completely different and much stronger person. I read the hepatitis C handbook and in short found out that it is a real killer. You recover from hepatitis B, but hepatitis C can kill. The incubation time can also be about 10 to 15 years so I figure I got it when I was injecting.

'It seems like it was a different person doing heroin, a different lifetime. But it's hit me again here now. I chant, I do a lot of training, I have acupuncture, take Chinese herbal medicine, and on the whole keep on top of the virus for most of the time. I'm not a born-again ex-drug addict. I don't drink because it is not a very good thing to drink with hepatitis C and because I am very comfortable with who I am now so I have no need to escape.

'With negative things in life, I think there are two ways to react, to curl up in the corner or fight it. I think if you go out fighting then you end up being stronger. One thing that scares me is that heroin was £70–£80 [$100–$115] a gram when I was into it heavily in 1982. Now I know you can get it for around £40 [$60] a gram, which is very cheap considering what people earn now. That frightens me.

'I've also got kids now. My daughter is almost ten, my son is nearly eight.

And I've got a four month old. I wouldn't tell them "Don't do that", but I think the more accurate information that gets out there the better. When I grew up there was a mystique about heroin - now it seems to be everywhere. There was a kind of forbidden glamour to it and I think it can only help if there are more facts and information so people have got the knowledge at their fingertips. Maybe the glamour thing will fade as well because everyone will know what it is about.

The *Oxford Handbook Of Clinical Medicine* records that a large proportion of the illness experienced by black-market heroin addicts is caused by wound infection, septicaemia, and infective endocarditis, all due to unhygienic injection technique.

'I'd never sit down and preach to my children. There's no point in just saying "Don't do it." My daughter is coming up to ten years old; I will talk to her at the right time and share my experience and insight. But I do sometimes wonder what will happen if there is a vacuum there; in some environments there can be a situation where there is vulnerability. If she starts hanging around in three or four years' time and hooks up with people who are starting to use drugs she might just be tempted to give it a go, so I think you can never stop it but being open, informative and honest can only help.

'I've enrolled her in stage school, which is giving her something creative and positive to do and I will give my son a similar opportunity soon. It's all about being as creative as you can be and if you are fulfilled positively then you don't need fulfilment from something like drugs.

'But how can you put it in one commercial? I remember the "Heroin Is A Life Sentence" advertisement poster. I remember that affecting me, thinking about it. The greatest ability most heroin users have is the power of avoidance and I think if the ad made me feel more worried, that probably gave me a better reason to go and score some more drugs.

'I'm not saying that they shouldn't do advertising. The more knowledge that is out there the better, but it needs to be targeted. Most of the people I knew who were taking heroin had a very negative view about life so there was really nothing that could be done to change anything. They certainly wouldn't take any notice of the ads.

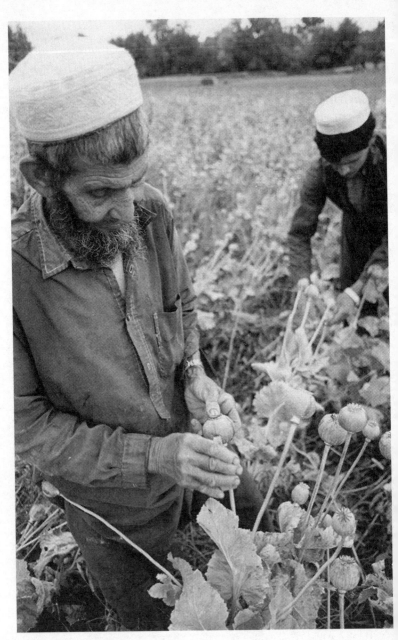

Opium poppy field, Afghanistan, 1998. A labourer scrapes the head of an opium poppy to extract opium paste in Taliban-controlled Jalalabad, eastern Afghanistan, during the annual bumper harvest. The interim authorities in Afghanistan began destroying poppy fields in 2002, despite violent protests from farmers.

The manufacture of opium in India, 1920.

'Looking back after almost 16 years, it's really hard to imagine that I could behave like that, it was so short-sighted. It's a waste of life. But, then again, I don't regret the experiences. I regret contracting hepatitis C, but I will not be defeated by this either. I think I am probably quite grateful for the whole experience, even though I wouldn't want to go back there because it taught me exactly how not to live – a crash course. One thing, it may sound obvious, but I get much more of a kick out of being really very alive now. That's probably why I am aware of health, keeping as fit as possible.

> What gives heroin an edge over other addictive drugs – including alcohol – from a filmmaker's point of view is the shock factor of needles: shooting up makes heroin use seem so more extreme than any other drug use.

'I kind of learnt in the most negative way how not to live. It's strange really because with a lot of musicians' careers, they can get more and more fucked up as time goes on. I've kind of done it in reverse order. I'm getting more together and happier as I go on, so from that respect I don't regret it. The one thing I'd change is the wasted time. I learnt lots from it, but I could have done something else.'

HEROIN STREET SLANG

Heroin's long history, cultural impact and prevalence among literary figures – with a poetic bent for adding to the argot – has ensured that it has probably more slang words associated with it than any other drug.

There are hundreds of different names for heroin (some of which are listed in the 'Street Names For Heroin' (see p 205), and it is unusual in that no gender has been successful in claiming it as its own. Both 'boy' and 'girl' are slang terms, as are the male and female names Henry, Harry, and Helen.

They are also constantly added to each year as a new generation of heroin users wants to personalize its use or take inspiration from its environment or culture. Thus, the tragic death of John Belushi in 1982 gave some heroin users the inspiration for another name to describe the speedball cocktail of heroin and cocaine, which led to the comic's demise. And, following the death of River Phoenix in 1993, some culturally aware addicts in north Hollywood and Santa Monica would, for as long as the actor's name continued to appear in newspapers, talk about 'falling' or 'swimming in the river' when they jacked up. Bart Simpson, the character from the TV show *The Simpsons*, has also been added to the slang list, as has TV host Jerry Springer.

With the drug's capacity to suddenly end life neither is it any coincidence that, more than any other drug, the slang draws on words associated with death ('heaven dust', 'dead on arrival', 'hell dust') or its methods ('bombs away'). Ecstasy is 'disco biscuits' and 'happiness', heroin is 'death trip'.

There is a definite geographical bias to the slang, which operates at a countrywide or even citywide level. Thus, 'chieva' or 'black tar', a type of

> 'I don't give a fuck what it's called as long as it's good shit. Come to think of it I often call it shit. Y'know. I'm doing some shit.' Mac, heroin user for 15 years

cheap heroin smuggled up from Mexico, and which has flooded west coast US cities, is popular around Haight-Ashbury in San Francisco, but will never be used in the estates around Moss Side in Manchester, where 'skag' has entered the vernacular. However, a London junkie in a Brixton squat may often prefer to use the more widespread 'smack'.

Even illegal drugs have brand names and heroin is no exception. In New York and many other US cities, dealers often branded the heroin they were supplying, even accompanying this with a distinctive logo on the $10 (£7) bags it was sold in. Some well-known 'brands' include names that are designed to appeal to the target consumer group by drumming home the dangerous outlaw status of the product: Homicide, Poison, Kill City, Last Payday, Body Bag, Lethal Injection, Silver Bullet.

By picking ever more outrageous names (see 'Junkie Slang', pp208-10) the dealers demonstrated they had learned a lesson from the media and advertising: shock sells and an established brand can lead to customer loyalty. These brands were traditionally sold from one spot and were recognizable because they would consistently have similar levels of purity and be cut with the same – non-narcotic – additives. In short, the addict knew what he was getting.

Raw ingredients and manufacturing method needed to produce 1kg (2¼lb) heroin:

- 10kg (22lb) opium;
- boil with water, filter and refine to produce morphine;
- add 17.5kg (38½lb) of assorted chemicals, including slaked lime, nicotine, activated charcoal, quinine, sodium carbonate, seconal, ammonium chloride, strychnine, and caffeine.

HEROIN MANUFACTURING, PURITY AND TYPE

Heroin is a semi-synthetic opiate produced from morphine. But its journey to New York's East Village or London's Soho starts as the milky sap of the opium poppy – *Papaver somniferum* – probably grown in a field somewhere in Afghanistan, Pakistan, or Myanmar.

Growers often use a technique called slash-and-burn farming to prepare the poppy fields for planting. After all the trees have been cut down and the vegetation has been cleared and burned, the farmers sow the poppy seeds.

Poppies can take about three months to mature, but harvesting will take place at different times of year depending on the part of the world they are being grown in. Just before reaching maturity, the poppy plant produces a flower, which indicates it is ready for harvest. After about a week, the flower petals fall off leaving a capsule.

Raw opium gum is harvested from this capsule. The surface of the capsule is cut or scored with a knife containing three or four small blades and the opium gum oozes out. The following day, the gum is scraped off the capsules with a flat tool. Each capsule is usually scored in this manner three to five times, or until no more gum exudes out.

After the harvesting process is complete, the capsules are cut from the stem, allowed to dry, and broken open so that the seeds inside the capsule can be used for next year's crop. Once the gum is collected, the farmer sets it out to dry for several days and then wraps it in plastic, or sometimes banana leaf if it has been harvested in Asia. Opium gum is dried, washed, boiled and reboiled to form the gumlike opium, which is ready for smoking. This also has a very long shelf life and can gain value over time.

Opium is used as a substitute for modern medicines in some remote areas, such as Southeast Asia, because few medical supplies are available. There are dozens of alkaloids in opium, but the principal ones of interest to recreational drug users are codeine and morphine. Codeine is often used in cough medicine or mild painkillers, but is not nearly as powerful as morphine and will usually only be of interest to drug abusers if their regular supply is cut.

Morphine is up to 1,000 per cent stronger than opium and is used medically as an analgesic in its pharmaceutical form as a suppository, pill or an injectable ampoule. Often the supply found on the streets is from medical stock following a burglary at a pharmacy and legally produced morphine pills are also smuggled from countries such as India.

Refining raw opium into heroin is a long, multi-step process. The opium gum is transported to a refinery and converted into morphine, which is dried and made into bricks ready for the chemical process to convert them into heroin. The morphine and acetic anhydride, used in the manufacture of film and synthetics, are then heated together at temperatures of 85°C (185°F) for six hours, which forms impure diacetylmorphine (heroin).

Water and chloroform are added to precipitate impurities before draining and the addition of sodium carbonate to solidify the heroin. Activated charcoal is used to filter the heroin out of the sodium carbonate solution and then it is purified with alcohol before being heated to evaporate off the alcohol.

PURITY

The refining process has been perfected to the point where heroin purity levels above 90 per cent can be achieved by the time the product leaves the refinery. Heroin's appearance can vary quite considerably depending on the manufacturing process and how much it is refined. Pure heroin is a white, odourless powder with a bitter taste.

However, because most heroin is illegally manufactured, levels of purity and colour can vary considerably depending on the production process involved and the substances with which the drug has been cut in order to maximize bulk and profit. The commonest non-narcotic adulterants include baking powder, chalk, glucose powder, caffeine, quinine, flour, talcum powder, powdered milk, or sugar. The colour can, therefore, vary dramatically from dark brown, through beige to pink and white.

1g of heroin seized in the UK in 1998 had an average purity of 37 per cent.

Pure heroin is rarely sold on the street. A bag – slang for a single dosage – may contain 100mg of powder, but only a fraction of that will be heroin; the remainder could be anything. In the 1970s the purity of heroin in a bag ranged from 1 to 10 per cent. However, in the mid-1990s drug enforcement agencies found that it was ranging between 15 and 99 per cent, and was routinely 50 per cent or more pure.

This was because dealers on the street, realising that higher levels of purity meant users could inhale or smoke the drug without the fear of HIV associated with intravenous needles, attempted to expand their market beyond the injecting junkies. The higher levels of purity also reflected the greater amounts of heroin available. In 2000, the US national average of heroin purity was 35 per cent, and in the UK in 2002 it was running at around 47 per cent across a purity range of 2 to 90 per cent.

Analysis of Drug Enforcement Administration (DEA) drug buys and seizures between 1981 and 1997 shows that purity increased from 7 per cent in 1981 for purchases of 0.5g or less, to 36 per cent in 1988 and rising to 56 per cent in 1997.

TYPE

Crude morphine is sometimes called heroin number one and the white to off-white, pale grey or dark brown, powdered or solid heroin base, prior to its conversion to the hydrochloric salt, is called heroin number two. A hard granular material, light brown, dark grey, red, or pink in colour, and containing between 25 and 45 per cent heroin hydrochloride and cut with other (sometimes non-narcotic) substances, is called heroin number three. This is also a smokable form of the drug.

The most highly refined heroin, with a purity level of 98 per cent heroin hydrochloride, no additives and white in colour, is heroin number four. Similarly, the medium-brown hard chunks of crude heroin produced without a purification process and between 40 and 60 per cent pure with a vinegary odour, are often referred to as 'brown heroin'.

One of the most crudely processed types of heroin is black tar, which is illicitly manufactured in Mexico and has become popular in the USA in recent years. This has a purity level of between 30 and 60 per cent heroin hydrochloride, is very dark brown or black coloured, and either sticky like roofing tar or hard and brittle like coal. Again there is a strong vinegary smell and it appears to melt when heated.

SYNTHETIC DRUGS

Heroin is manufactured, but its roots are clearly from the opium poppy. However, many other drugs exhibit similar effects but don't rely on the poppy for their source material. These are called synthetics and are mostly produced legally for medical use, but are illegally traded on the streets.

Many users of these clinical opioids, which often have recognizable brand names, believe they are safer than heroin simply because they are manufactured in licensed laboratories. Sometimes, however, these 'designer drugs' are produced in illegal laboratories and are often more dangerous and potent than heroin if misused.

FENTANYL

Known on the street as 'china white' and one of the most commonly known opioid analogues, fentanyl was introduced in 1968 by a Belgian pharmaceutical company as a synthetic narcotic to be used as an analgesic in surgical procedures because of its minimal effects on the heart. Fentanyl is particularly dangerous because it is 50 times more potent than heroin and can stop respiration rapidly, although the euphoria is less than morphine. This is not a problem during surgical procedures because machines are used to help patients breathe; however, on-the-street users have been found dead with the needle used to inject the drug still in their arms.

DEXTROMORAMIDE
An opioid analgesic used for the treatment of severe pain. It is short-acting and causes less sedation than morphine. Dextromoramide is available in tablet form or as a suppository and may cause depression of breathing.

ACETAMINOPHEN-OXYCODONE
This is a combination of two different types of pain medicine used to treat moderate to severe pain. Generic acetaminophen-oxycodone tablets and capsules are available, but the powerful painkiller is only available on prescription and normally dispensed only to the terminally ill. Oxycodone, known as 'percs' on the street, has been dubbed hillbilly heroin and has been responsible for hundreds of deaths in the USA. Essentially a synthetic form of morphine, the tablets are crushed together to provide a hit, and experts say it is more potent and more addictive than heroin. The small white tablets can be swallowed whole, crushed and snorted or mixed with water and injected. Each tablet costs £5-20 ($7-30) depending on its strength.

PETHIDINE
Pethidine is an analgesic and an anti-spasmodic, which is a drug that helps people relax. It's a similar drug to morphine, which midwives often prescribe and administer during childbirth. It is given as an injection and often combined with another drug – an anti-emetic – to control sickness. For drug abusers it can produce a short buzz.

DIHYDROCODEINE

The opioid dihydrocodeine (DHC) is frequently used as an analgesic and is one of the most commonly prescribed painkillers in the UK, but can cause severe constipation.

BUPRENORPHINE

Buprenorphine is available by prescription (under the brand name Subutex) as a treatment for heroin. It has been found to be effective in preventing the need to use heroin and also in helping people to withdraw. But buprenorphine, which is also prescribed to treat severe pain, became a real problem in the 1980s when it was used illegally as a heroin substitute on the streets.

PENTAZOCINE

The effort to find an effective analgesic that is less dependence-producing led to the development of pentazocine. Introduced as an analgesic in 1967, it has frequently been encountered in the illicit trade, usually in combination with tripelennamine. Can give users morphine-like effects if the tablets are dissolved and injected, however some users have also reported that it can cause hallucinations.

DIPIPANONE

Dipipanone hydrochloride is medically used as a painkiller and can be taken orally or injected after it has been crushed and dissolved in warm water. It is a very strong painkiller (often prescribed to cancer patients) with definite physical dependent-forming potential as it causes strong withdrawal symptoms and signs similar to heroin and morphine use. However, the high silicon content of the drug means that veins can quickly silt up, causing circulation problems.

METHADONE

Synthetic methadone was devised by German chemists during World War II at the German group IG Farbenindustrie. Also called 'dollies' by abusers, methadone works well taken orally and can be effective for over 20 hours. Prescribed as a substitute for heroin, it comes in several different formats: tablets, 10mg ampoules, a linctus, and a liquid green, yellow or brown mixture, which usually contains glucose and chloroform water to dissuade injectors.

HEROIN COCKTAILS

Drug users don't usually confine their choice of narcotic to just one. Heroin dependants are no different. Most are poly-drug or multiple substance abusers.

Some heroin addicts use a multitude of different narcotics, but alcohol, tranquillizers, barbiturates, amphetamines, and cocaine are the most popular. The junkie will use them when his regular supply of dope is cut or his dealer is out of town, to heighten the effect of heroin and, sometimes, to help him cope during withdrawal.

Mixing heroin with other drugs can have two effects: it can increase the buzz and the danger. Pairing dope with barbiturates, tranquillizers or alcohol can cause severe depression of the central nervous system and lead to coma and death.

Also, the combination of heroin and alcohol often causes vomiting, which is particularly dangerous if the mix of the drugs has caused unconsciousness. Cocaine and heroin are the best-known double act: the speedball. The ultimate stimulant paired with the number one soporific.

HEROIN PRODUCTION

The global supply of illicit opium, the raw material for heroin, has varied enormously in the last century. But the real growth in supply – to meet the demand for the drug – kicked off in the 1980s when production levels tripled from around 1,000 tonnes in 1981 to 3,000 tonnes less than a decade later.

By the 1990s production levels hit the 5,000 tonne mark and remained relatively stable until 2000, although a bumper Afghan harvest of 4,600 tonnes in 1999 helped boost worldwide production to 5,800 tonnes. Despite this increase in production, the global area under opium poppy cultivation in 1999 was almost 20 per cent less than in 1990 when over 250,000ha (617,500 acres) was under cultivation. This suggests that cultivation techniques had improved over the decade and producers were able to gain better yields per hectare.

In terms of the global heroin market, Afghanistan and Myanmar (formerly Burma) are in a league of their own. They are by far the biggest producers of opium, accounting for over 90 per cent of the opium produced in 2000. Figures for 1999 suggest that Afghanistan alone had a total area under cultivation of 91,583ha (226,210 acres) and, by the late 1990s, Afghanistan was estimated to be the source of 75 per cent of the world's heroin and 90 per cent of the supply that found its way to the UK.

> 'You'd be stupid not to grow opium. If the Americans give us some money, we'll stop planting poppy. If they don't, we'll carry on.' Afghan farmer

With such a monopoly on the global market, natural disasters such as droughts, improving law enforcement, a new government regime and – in the case of Afghanistan – a war could have a massive effect on the world's supply.

AFGHANISTAN

Afghan's opium harvest in 2000 was only about 3,300 tonnes and led directly to reduced global production levels of heroin. However, by the beginning of 2002, experts were warning that with the overthrow of the Islamic fundamentalist Taliban regime, opium – and therefore heroin – production would increase dramatically.

Opium has flourished in Afghanistan's southern desert region and northern provinces since the times of Alexander the Great. The poppies are well suited to the rugged terrain and arid climate, requiring little water or attention, and making them easier and cheaper to cultivate than wheat and other crops.

The poppy crop and trade in heroin has thrived through countless regimes, from the 1933–73 reign of King Zahir Shah, through the Soviet occupation during the 1980s, the bloody years of the Mojaheddin and the rise of the fundamentalist Taliban in the 1990s.

The Taliban surprised illegal producers and traffickers in 2000 when the government's leader, Mullah Mohammed Omar, issued an edict outlawing opium production in Afghanistan. As the world's largest producer of heroin throughout the 1990s the Taliban, which had seized control of the country in 1996, had earned millions from the heroin trade because drug traffickers were required to pay the Taliban's commerce ministry a 10 per cent tax on cultivation profits and 20 per cent on smuggling profits.

Afghan farmers were forced to turn to planting other, less profitable, crops or vineyards in place of their poppy fields and only areas under the control of the opposition Northern Alliance continued to produce opium. The result was that poppy cultivation fell to just 7,706ha (19,034 acres) in 2001 from 82,515ha (203,812 acres) the year before.

Some experts believed the Taliban may have been attempting to strangle supply and drive up the price of opium on the international market. This would have had the effect of significantly increasing the cost of a bag of heroin on a New York or London street. The economics supported this theory: in September 2001, when there was no prospect of a fresh crop under the Taliban, 1kg (2¼lb) of opium cost between \$570 (£390) and \$655 (£450).

The 11 September 2001 attacks on the twin towers of New York's World Trade Center changed that. The USA traced the terrorists' network to Osama bin Laden's al-Qaeda network, which was being harboured by the Taliban in Afghanistan. The war against terrorism that followed, and the subsequent fall of the Taliban regime at the end of 2001, meant the Afghan farmers reverted to their more lucrative crop: opium. The motivation wasn't hard to find. In the 1990s the opium trade was estimated to be worth around \$98 million (£68 million) to Afghan growers and a farmer, fresh after the crippling conflict with the defeated Taliban, could have expected to make thousands trading with Pakistani and Iranian buyers if he replanted his wheat fields with opium at the end of 2001.

In 1999, the worldwide production of opium was 5,800 tonnes.

This was despite a new ban on poppy cultivation issued by the Afghan Interim Administration (AIA) on 17 January 2002. Significantly, with the prospect of future harvests in 2002 and beyond, opium prices tumbled to between \$407 (£280) and \$423 (£295) in January 2002.

The future recovery of the opium and heroin trade following the war was also expected to be quick. Research showed that Afghan farmers were turning back to their main cash crop in 2002. Prior to the opium harvesting seasons (from April to May in southern and eastern Afghanistan, and from June to August in the northern region) the United Nations Drug Control Programme (UNDCP) conducted a survey of expected opium cultivation for 2002.

The Opium Poppy Survey pre-assessment, published in February 2002, estimated that opium poppy cultivation could cover between 45,000ha (110,000 acres) and 65,000ha (160,000 acres) in 2002, just short of 1998 levels when 63,674ha (157,275 acres) were under poppies. Based on an average yield of 41kg (90lb) per hectare (2½ acres), the UN researchers estimated that the 2002 crop production in Afghanistan could reach 2,700 tonnes, enough to make 270 tonnes of heroin.

Consequently, in early 2002, law enforcement and intelligence agencies were warning Europe and the USA that they faced potentially huge increases in heroin trafficking because of massive and unchecked replanting of the opium crop. The expectation at the time was that that year's crop would be equivalent to the bumper one of 1999, which had yielded 4,600 tonnes of raw opium.

Although the AIA threatened to confiscate land and prosecute farmers cultivating opium, UK government officials and drug experts privately conceded that the Afghan decree would only succeed in tandem with massive international financial backing and expert support. With a fragile political climate it was also difficult for the West to pile too much pressure on the AIA for fear of destabilizing it; most of the opium was grown in the Pashtun-dominated south and east of Afghanistan, and if the Pashtuns were isolated it was feared that this may dissuade them from backing the administration.

One radical solution proposed was for European governments to buy the poppy crop, but this would have been highly controversial as well as costly. There was also recognition that providing aid and substitute crops to poor farmers would not necessarily solve the problem because any attempt to control the trade would be resisted by local warlords.

Finally, in a bid to undermine the replanting, an ambitious US- and

EU-sponsored programme designed to destroy Afghanistan's opium crop was launched in April 2002. The AIA agreed a plan that offered farmers £175 ($255) for every *jirib* (about 2 sq km/¾ sq mile) of opium poppies they destroyed. In a good year, one *jirib* could produce 16kg (35lb) of raw opium. The AIA said, 'The holy religion of Islam is categorical about the evil impact of drugs. We are determined to eradicate the current poppy crop.'

In the mid-'90s, the World Health Organization estimated that 40 per cent of recent AIDS cases internationally had been caused by drug users sharing injecting equipment.

The European Commission also offered to support the move. Brussels pledged £17.5 million ($25.5 million) to help poppy-growing areas find alternative sources of income. EU External Affairs Commissioner Chris Patten blamed Afghan-sourced heroin for 'devastating' lives and funding organized crime. He added, 'Beating drugs helps beat terrorism and will help Afghans have a brighter future.'

MYANMAR

Myanmar, formerly Burma, is part of Southeast Asia's infamous 'Golden Triangle', which also comprises parts of Laos and Thailand. It is also the world's second largest producer of illicit opium and in 1999 had 89,500ha (221,000 acres) under cultivation.

Illegal drugs have had a long history of supply and manufacture in the country, although it was only in the last decade of the 20th century that Myanmar became a global capital for opium growing and heroin production, helping to fuel the number of addicts worldwide.

The political regimes in place prior to the 1988 State Peace and Development Council (SPDC) junta had not overtly supported the illicit heroin trade. But a significant proportion of the massive income derived from heroin production had flowed to the ruling government, the army or the hundreds of competing ethnic opposition groups. In the early 1990s there were around 135 ethnic groups, each with their own states and armies and, with the Burmese Communist Party and other opium-trade protection gangs, controlled vast swathes of the heroin-producing lands.

Also, any measures aimed at strangling supplies were often undermined.

Anti-drug funds flowing from the West were historically diverted by successive Burmese regimes to other uses, such as counter-insurgency measures to quell ethnic groups demanding independence.

However, the manufacture and supply of heroin in the country boomed following the bloody takeover of the country by the Law and Order Restoration Council (renamed the SPDC in November 1997) in 1988. Drug lords, who had close links to Burma's army dictators, were able to act almost with impunity, and there was a lack of commitment from the government towards stamping out narcotic trafficking and the money laundering that followed it.

There were some successes, such as the surrender of drug warlord Khun Sa. He was the leader of the southern Shan State and on America's 'Most Wanted' list following an indictment on narcotics racketeering charges in a New York court. But some commentators argued that his arrest was largely a public relations exercise and that the government was practically a trade partner in the cultivation, supply and manufacture of illicit drugs.

This was largely confirmed when a ceasefire was called in the late 1990s. This essentially gave the opposition parties free rein, leading to massive increases in the opium harvest and purer forms of heroin on the street. Between 1988 and 1997 the average purity of heroin shot up from 34 per cent to 62.5 per cent. The US State Department stated in its 2000 International Narcotics Control Strategy Report: '...the ceasefire agreements have permitted former insurgents to continue their involvement in narcotics cultivation and trafficking activities.'

OTHER MAJOR HEROIN PRODUCERS

After Afghanistan and Myanmar, the Lao PDR, Colombia, and Mexico produced the largest quantities of illegal opium in 1999. They had 22,550ha (55,700 acres), 7,500ha (18,500 acres) and 3,600ha (8,900 acres) of poppies under cultivation, respectively.

Opium production in Mexico and Latin and Central American countries such as Peru and Venezuela, was mainly destined for the US heroin market at the beginning of 2002, with Colombia replacing Southeast Asia as a prime source of the drug in the late 1990s; 65 per cent of the heroin seized in the USA during this period was sourced to Colombia.

Other major opium producers in 2002 included Pakistan, Thailand, and Vietnam. However, production of opium and heroin fell in Southeast Asia in the late 1990s, and Thailand and Pakistan also drastically cut cultivation, with the latter reducing the number of hectares under the poppy from 7,500ha (18,500 acres) in 1990 to just 3,000ha (7,400 acres) in 1999.

China, the largest producer of opium in the inter-war period (1919-39), Guatemala in central America, Lebanon, Iran, and Egypt, which all had fairly sizeable fields under cultivation, had also reduced production to practically zero by 2000.

HEROIN SUPPLY AND TRAFFICKING ROUTES

Once the opium crop has been harvested, raw opium or heroin is trafficked across the globe to the main drug centres. Sometimes this can involve long and complex routes facilitating the use of every imaginable mode of transport – from donkey to aircraft.

Trafficking of heroin and the main routes via which it is shipped can be traced by the number and pattern of seizures. Generally seizures of illicit drugs have increased, with 170 countries around the world reporting drug seizures in 1997/98 compared to just 120 in 1980/81.

However, heroin is not the world's most widely trafficked drug. Of those

One-third of all heroin seized in the European Union is destined for the UK.

countries that successfully seized drugs in 1997/98, only 91 per cent reported finding opiate substances, including heroin, compared with 98 per cent of the countries that reported finding cannabis products in their hauls.

However, along with the increase in the number of countries reporting seizures, heroin trafficking has shown an upward trend over the last 30 years. Less than five tonnes of the drug was seized each year between 1975 and 1980, but by 1998 this had increased to nearly 35 tonnes.

Of seizures of heroin and morphine in 1987/88, 72 per cent were made in Asia, with some 42 per cent discovered in Iran, reflecting its proximity to the trade routes coming out of Afghanistan. As befits its status as the

Sculpted head of Alexander the Great, King of Macedonia, 356–323 BC. In 460 BC, the father of medicine, Hippocrates, acknowledged opium's use as a narcotic and styptic in treating internal diseases. By AD 400, Alexander the Great had introduced opium to Persia and India, and Arabic traders were shipping the poppy to China.

Smokers in the Lascars' Room, an opium den in London's East End, 1873. A Lascar sits on a bench heating a long pipe over a fire.

Boiling and testing opium in China, 1880. By the mid-17th century, opium had become the main commodity of British trade with China, its use thus taking root in the Far East. By 1839, it had also caused a war between the British and Chinese. The East India Company had enjoyed a monopoly on shipping opium from Bengal into China, obtaining a revenue of £2 million ($2.9 million).

world's largest opium producer, Afghanistan is the main supplier of heroin to a wide range of countries, from neighbours such as Iran and Pakistan to Western European markets, including France and the UK.

The UN warned in early 2002 that unless measures were successful to stop the harvest of that year's Afghan opium crop, then the 'best ever opportunity' to suffocate the illegal trade would be lost. The Taliban ban on poppy growing in Afghanistan, introduced in July 2000 and coupled with severe droughts in 2001, reduced Afghanistan's opium yield by 91 per cent in 2001. It was thought, however, to have had little effect on trafficking throughout Europe because traders had stockpiled significant amounts of heroin along their supply routes.

Between 1987 and 1988 Europe accounted for about 23 per cent of worldwide seizures, at over 10,000kg (22,000lb), with most taking place in western countries including Turkey. The Americas accounted for about 3.7 per cent of heroin and morphine seizures in 1997/98.

In 1999, over seven tonnes of heroin were seized in the EU, of which one-third was accountable to the United Kingdom. Heroin seized in the EU comes mainly from the so-called 'Golden Crescent' - a mountainous area including Iran, Afghanistan, and Pakistan - followed by the Golden Triangle routed via Turkey, the Balkans and The Netherlands. However, after 2000 smugglers moved their routes

One kilo (21/4lb) of heroin costs £24,000 in the UK and $35,000 in the USA, compared to £850 ($1,200) in Pakistan.

north and US drug enforcement agencies reported that the number of heroin shipments from Afghanistan through the central Asian states to Russia had increased; Tajikistan was a favourite destination. In 2002 one heroin trade expert estimated that only 20-30 per cent of heroin was shipped to Europe via the usual Iranian-Turkish route.

At EU level, heroin seizures increased up until 1991/92 and then stabilized. The number of heroin seizures has grown steadily in Luxembourg, Portugal, and Sweden since 1985, while marked decreases have been reported since 1996/97 in Austria, Belgium, Denmark, France, Germany, and Spain. In every member state, the quantities seized fluctuated over the period. In 1999, marked decreases in the quantities of heroin seized were reported in Austria,

France, Greece, Ireland and The Netherlands, while in Italy and Spain there were large increases in the amount of heroin seized.

Seizures in the UK increased by more than 80 per cent in 1999, which is significant because the UK already accounted for around 30 per cent of all heroin and morphine seizures in the EU during 1997/98, more than The Netherlands (about 20 per cent) and Germany (12 per cent). In 2001 it was reported that Afghanistan and the Golden Crescent was the source of 90 per cent of the heroin reaching Britain's streets.

> There are 227,000 regular heroin users in Britain, consuming over 30 tonnes of heroin each year. DrugScope 2002

The impact of the drug trade from Myanmar has been felt by its neighbours, Bangladesh, China, India, Singapore, and Thailand. They all experienced increased incidents of heroin seizures, a rapidly expanding community of addicts and a rise in HIV in the 1990s. In a 1998 survey throughout the northern state of Kachin, over 90 per cent of heroin users tested HIV positive.

Turkey has always been an important part of the heroin map and, between 1990/91 and 1997/98, heroin and morphine seizures in the country have increased by more than 10 per cent to over 3,000kg (6,600lb). In the late 1990s Turkey, midway between the producer countries Afghanistan and Pakistan and the European market, also emerged as a final destination and transit territory for acetic anhydride, one of heroin's major precursor chemicals, which is manufactured throughout Europe and shipped to Asia.

The majority of heroin crossing Turkey is shipped along the Balkan route to its final destination, although some new developing markets emerged in Eastern Europe in the late 1990s and many countries along the main trafficking routes – such as Iran, Pakistan, and Central Asian countries – became bigger buyers.

Pakistan, which shares a border with Afghanistan, remains an important player in the global heroin market despite a decline in seizures during the 1990s because of a reduction in domestic production and large scale re-routing of heroin traffic via Iran. However, Pakistan still accounted for 9 per cent of all worldwide heroin and morphine seizures in 1997/98 and its geographical importance was demonstrated in 1999 when large amounts of

Afghan's bumper opium poppy harvest of 4,600 tonnes were shipped across the country, leading to an increase in seizures.

India, the world's largest legal opium producer, has improved controls over manufacturing and cut seizures of heroin and morphine by more than 60 per cent between 1990/91 and 1997/98, with seizures in 1997/98 between 1,000kg and 3,000kg (2,200lb and 6,600lb).

Around 16 per cent of global seizures in 1997/98 were made in Southeast Asia, an area incorporating the notorious Golden Triangle, traditionally one of the main outlets for heroin. However, there were some radical changes in trafficking patterns in the 1990s with Thailand's importance as a main route in the area diminishing. By 1997/98 Thailand only accounted for around 5 per cent of all seizures of opiates in Southeast Asia, compared to almost 60 per cent in the late 1980s.

The Asia-based criminal networks supplying the USA have virtually been squeezed out of the market, although there is evidence that Southeast Asian heroin is being smuggled into the United States in smaller multigram or multikilogram amounts by couriers or mail and package delivery services.

Its place in the league of suppliers has been taken by China, where heroin was smuggled directly from Myanmar for export to the USA, usually via Hong Kong. However, poor weather conditions in 1999 reduced production, and seizures in China were down 30 per cent that year.

The US heroin market is supplied entirely from foreign sources of opium produced in four distinct geographical areas: South America, Mexico, Southeast Asia and Southwest Asia. In 2000, 1,415kg (3,119lb) of heroin was seized in the USA under the Federal-wide Drug Seizure System, which includes the DEA, FBI and US Customs. This was significantly up on the 1,239kg (2,732lb) seized in the previous year.

Trafficking patterns have changed significantly since the mid-1990s when Southeast Asia was the main supplier for the North American markets and accounted for around 3 per cent of global heroin and morphine seizures in 1997/98. By 1999, however, Southeast Asia accounted for only around 10 per cent of heroin seized in the USA, and Southeast Asia accounted for just 6 per cent.

The flow of South American heroin began to increase dramatically around 1993 when Colombia-based gangs, already in control of the cocaine trade, expanded into heroin. They quickly saturated the USA heroin markets using Dominican distribution rings and by providing low-cost, high-purity heroin. They also employed surefire marketing tactics such as providing free samples of heroin in cocaine shipments, and using brand names to build their client base and customer loyalty.

TABLE 2.1: SEIZURES OF HEROIN AND MORPHINE (KG), 1994–8

	1994	1998
Iran	13,767	25,186
China	4,086	7,504
Turkey	2,474	5,406
Pakistan	6,444	3,364
The Netherlands	246	2,072
United States	1,333	1,581
United Kingdom	776	1,386
Italy	1,152	706
Germany	1,590	686
India	1,062	674
Hungary	812	635
Thailand	1,295	508
Myanmar	233	499
Turkmenistan	12	495
Spain	824	444

Note: 1kg = 2¼lb)

Source: UNDCP, *Global Illicit Drug Trends*, 2000

The South American and Latin American countries supplied 75 per cent of US heroin in 1997, 65 per cent in 1998 and around 60 per cent in 1999. Virtually all of the six tonnes of heroin produced in Colombia during 1998 was believed to have been shipped to the US market, and Colombian heroin began to dominate the streets of east coast cities such as New York and Washington in 1999. The heroin trade in Colombia was in the hands of many independent trafficking groups and the drug is smuggled mainly in quantities of 1kg (2¼lb) or 2kg (4½lb) by couriers on commercial airlines.

Criminal organizations based in Nigeria and West Africa, with drug connections in Southeast and Southwest Asia, also distributed heroin to some major cities in the United States, particularly the Chicago area. Similarly, nearly all heroin produced in Mexico between 1999 and 2001 was destined for US distribution. Mexican heroin, which accounted for 24 per cent of US seizures in 1999, became more popular in southwestern US cities such as San Diego and Los Angeles.

Evidence suggests that trafficking organizations from Mexico were attempting to produce higher-purity heroin in the late 1990s. A 1997 analysis of Mexican heroin distributed in the USA revealed purity levels of 30 to 60 per cent, with some samples reaching levels of more than 70 per cent.

HEROIN INJECTING, SMOKING, AND SNORTING

'Smoking is not a very cost-effective way of using heroin because, quite literally, most of it goes up in smoke. If you are going to become a heroin user on a regular basis then you'd have to go on the needle.'

- Harry Shapiro, communications director at UK drugs information resource DrugScope

Heroin is a very adaptable drug. Many narcotics can only be popped as pills or snorted. Heroin, however, can be administered in a variety of ways with different effects. It can be sniffed, smoked, swallowed, or injected. These methods can involve different techniques. Heroin can be smoked though a water pipe or normal pipe (often glass), mixed with a marijuana joint, inhaled as smoke through a straw (chasing the dragon), snorted as a powder (commonly through a straw), or dissolved in water and injected under the skin, into muscles or intravenously (into a vein).

Sniffing or snorting is done in the same way as cocaine users do Charlie. The heroin is chopped with a blade, razor or credit card, drawn into lines and then snorted up one nostril with the aid of a rolled-up banknote or tube. The bitter flavour of heroin can put users off this method, and sniffing largely remains the preserve of the cocaine addict.

Swallowing heroin is pretty rare because it is an inefficient way of delivering a rush. The stomach converts heroin into morphine and the liver does a good job of breaking down the morphine before it can have an effect.

With smoking, a small amount of H is placed on a piece of aluminium foil and a flame held beneath it. As the drug is heated it turns black and wriggles like a snake. The resulting fumes are sucked up into the nose with the help of a tube.

TABLE 2.2: HEROIN ADMISSIONS BY ROUTE OF ADMINISTRATION, 1993–8

	1993	1994	1995	1996	1997	1998
Heroin admissions (000s)	193	212	221	217	221	230
Route of administration			%			
Injection	74.2	73.2	69.6	69.4	67.5	66.2
Inhalation	22.5	23.3	26.7	26.4	27.9	29.0
Smoking	1.7	1.9	2.2	2.4	2.7	2.7
Other	1.7	1.6	1.6	1.7	1.8	2.0

Source: Substance Abuse and Mental Health Services Administration (SAMHSA)

INJECTING

Injection can be done in three ways:

- **Skin Popping** – The common name given to subcutaneous injection, which targets the fatty tissue lying just beneath the skin (usually in the buttocks, stomach or thighs);
- **Intramuscular Injection** – When the user targets his large muscle groups, normally in the thigh, buttocks or the top of the arms;
- **Intravenous Injection** – Also called mainlining, which targets veins.

Injection is still the most popular method, although it is becoming less so. A Substance Abuse and Mental Health Services Administration (SAMHSA) Treatment Episode Data Set (TEDS) found that, in 1998, 66 per cent of people treated for heroin addiction were injectors. This number had declined from 74 per cent in 1993 (see Table 2.2 above).

Typically, a heroin abuser will inject up to four times in a day. Mainlining directly into veins provides the greatest intensity and most rapid onset of euphoria (between seven and eight seconds), while intramuscular injection or skin popping produces a slower high, sometimes taking as long as eight minutes before the onset of euphoria.

When heroin is snorted or smoked, peak effects are usually much longer – taking between 10 and 15 minutes – and, in addition to a slower 'rush', these methods don't create the intensity of intravenous injection. All forms of heroin administration are addictive.

Intramuscular or subcutaneous injection was used almost exclusively in Britain in the early part of the 20th century. But intravenous use, which was more common in the USA eventually spread to the UK and Europe around the 1950s possibly because injection is the most practical and efficient way of administering low-purity heroin.

Intravenous use carries with it all of the primary health risks facing heroin users. Mainlining means that any toxic substances cut with the drug are shot directly into the blood, leading to abscesses, blood poisoning or worse.

In the process of injecting heroin users will usually place a small amount of the drug (anything up to the size of a pea, although it varies enormously depending on the addict) on to a spoon. If they are fixing with brown they will add a drop of citric or ascorbic acid and water to help dissolve the heroin. Sometimes vinegar and lemon juice are more easily available for the junkie, but can cause infection.

The mix is heated over a naked flame from a lighter until it dissolves. Once the heroin has melted and cooled it can be drawn up into a syringe and injected. Often a small swab of cotton wool or a filter from a cigarette will also be used to screen some of the toxins in the heroin, but bacteria can still be drawn into the hypodermic.

At the start of a habit, the needle user will inject in the most accessible veins, which are the main arteries located in the inner portion of the arm near the elbow joint. Usually, a right-handed person will inject in the left arm and a left-handed person into the right arm. Sometimes injectors will also pump their arms or use a tourniquet such as a belt or tie to make a bigger target of the vein.

Commonly referred to as 'the ditch', this arm injection site may not be noticeable during the early stages of heroin use if the drug is only being injected up to three times a week. However, as the user's addiction and habit develops, multiple injections over 24 hours are common and the needle marks on the veins will turn into tiny scabs. These scabs may extend several centimetres along the top of the vein and are called tracks.

The more often the user shoots up the more likely it is that they will need to graduate to a number of other injection sites, such as the leg, because repeated injection into the same vein can cause it to collapse or blow out. After using the veins in the arms and the arteries behind the knees, addicts will move on to the veins on the back of hands, and some addicts have also shot up in the neck's jugular vein. As the tracks become more noticeable the heroin user will also self-consciously keep his arms and legs covered at all times to hide his addiction. Even if the heroin user does eventually kick their habit, the tracks can leave scarring – a permanent reminder of heroin.

FIRST PERSON
LISA S, HEROIN ADDICT

'I started with a needle in the 1970s. I was 17 at the time and didn't know there was anything but mainlining. Also, I never smoked, never have, which is pretty unusual I guess with heroin users. My boyfriend at the time was a user and he showed me what to do. He fixed me up with my first shot and I thought it was wonderful.

'You hear all these stories about people feeling bad and puking up. But that was not my experience. I thought it was really wonderful. I suppose I'd been around drugs quite a lot then and had tried most of everything, especially acid. I had the best two or three years of my life. Fantastic music, great gigs, and smack.

'There'd be some bad times where we couldn't get hold of any dope for a few days and then I couldn't cope. That was dreadful. I was working on the tills in a market, just a small corner convenience store really, but I just couldn't face it without a fix. I'd ring in at least once a week and tell them I was ill. I don't know if they suspected anything. I kept myself pretty presentable and it wasn't like there were many heroin addicts around then. I could fix myself and did sometimes, but mostly my boyfriend did it.

'What happened then was he had a terrible motorbike accident and was in hospital for nearly a year. The doctors got him off heroin while he was there and I started to visit him less and less because I was still doing it. Although, by this time my health was really shot. I'd miss veins and get bruising all over my arm. Then I met someone else who was also dealing a bit. He moved in and, although I knew he was ripping me off, we stuck together because of the dope I knew he could always get.

'By this time my veins were pretty fucked up. I was spilling loads of blood all over the place and the hits seemed to be becoming less and less. I just didn't get that feeling back. I don't know if it was the quality of the dope or something. So we both started doing cocaine as well. Around this time I realised I couldn't keep a lid on everything. I'd lost the supermarket job and was just doing odd shifts in a local bar.

'Then my first boyfriend came out of hospital and I saw him one night in another pub. Even though his leg was a bit fucked, he looked really good. He was completely clean and he'd been away on holiday somewhere and was suntanned, and that's what I noticed most, his skin and hair. Also, the idea of going away had never been something we would have done. In fact, I hardly recognized him because he'd been a user ever since I'd met him.

'He didn't give me any lecture, in fact I can't remember if we even spoke, but something clicked then and I knew I had to move out of the flat with the dealer. It probably took another two years to get off the gear altogether, but I've been clean since.'

SNIFFING AND SMOKING

In the 1980s and 1990s there was a shift in heroin use patterns in some US cities and the UK: from injection to sniffing and smoking. Evidence suggests that heroin snorting is widespread in cities and countries where high-purity heroin is available. According to a report by the USA Drug Enforcement Administration (DEA) the purity of 1oz (28g) of street heroin rose from just 34 per cent in 1990 to 66 per cent in 1993. Snorting heroin is now the most widely reported means of taking heroin among users admitted for drug treatment in Newark, Chicago, and New York.

A US Drug Abuse Warning Network (DAWN) survey, conducted by SAMHSA, also found that between 1988 and 1993 the number of hospital emergency department visits related to snorting heroin jumped by 470 per cent from 1,100 to 6,000. However, this still constituted only around 13 per cent of the total number of heroin-related hospital emergencies.

Along with the shift in abuse patterns to new, young users lured by inexpensive, high-purity heroin that can be snorted or smoked, heroin has also been appearing in more affluent communities. In the past, groups such as students and business executives have traditionally avoided the drug because of negative images of needles and the stigma associated with track marks. However, smoking and snorting bypasses this. The SAMHSA TEDS survey showed that people who inhaled heroin tended to be younger. In 1993, 47 per cent of admissions for heroin inhalation were under 30 years. Only 23 per cent of those injecting heroin at the time of admission were under 30. By 1998, however, 27 per cent of those reporting heroin injection were under 30, compared with 35 per cent of those admitted for inhaling heroin. The obvious explanation is that inhalers eventually graduated to becoming injectors.

> Research suggests that, in England and Wales, a hard core of black-market users is responsible for some £1.5 billion ($2.2 billion) worth of burglary, theft and shoplifting each year – they are stealing £3.5 million ($5.1 million) worth of property a day.

Snorting and smoking is also more appealing to a new group of users because these methods eliminate the fear of acquiring syringe-borne diseases such as HIV and hepatitis B and C.

When smoked, heroin is heated on a small piece of baking foil and the fumes inhaled through a tube. Chasing the dragon – so called because the smoke spiralling off the aluminium foil looks like a dragon's tail – became popular in 1980s Britain when fairly large supplies of heroin were flooding council estates in cities such as Liverpool, Manchester, and London.

A 1992 AIDS conference in Amsterdam suggested that nearly two-thirds of heroin users chase the dragon. Some of these smokers will graduate to shooting up, but many will prefer to chase because they feel it is safer and may also enjoy the effects of heroin more.

Those that do chase will defend the method because the lungs provide a natural barrier to the toxic substances before the heroin is absorbed into the bloodstream. However, this poses another set of problems: aluminium kitchen foil, one of the most popular foils used by the smokers, is often backed by a thin layer of plastic to prevent rusting and make it easier to roll. In its normal kitchen use slightly toxic fumes are not harmful, but anyone chasing the dragon could also be inhaling plastic directly into their lungs. At the same time, there may also be fumes from the aluminium itself if it is heated to a very high temperature.

Air passages can contract and become irritated by these fumes and all smoking, whether tobacco or heroin, will put the smoker's lungs at risk of bronchial complaints. Heroin use will also suppress people's need to cough up phlegm and this can then accumulate and lead to pneumonia.

In addition to this, research suggests that some types of heroin – mostly from Afghanistan and Pakistan – are more suitable for chasing than others. The levels of heroin contained in the fumes will also vary greatly depending on the type of heroin and what it has been cut with. For example, fumes from Turkish heroin have been found to be three times more potent than those from Chinese heroin. Heroin cut with caffeine also appears to increase the levels of the drug in the fumes because the non-narcotic will evaporate at a much lower temperature. However, if the heroin is cut with other common ingredients such as glucose, paracetamol, lactose and strychnine, the percentage of heroin in the smoke reduces considerably.

There is certainly less equipment necessary for chasing the dragon. The mainliner will have his 'works'. He needs to be able to cook up the dope, often using something like a rubber hose to tie off his arm and, most importantly, a working sterile syringe with a sharp needle. The smoker only needs to rip off a piece of kitchen roll or buy some chocolate wrapped in silver foil – both easily available, cheap and reusable. However, there is some skill necessary with chasing. The user needs to be quick with his tube because if the heroin is heated too quickly smoke will be lost.

Chasing the dragon has one final, but important, advantage over mainlining: smokers can test the quality of the dope they are using. Mainliners will dissolve the dope, fix a shot and inject it. Only then will they know how pure the heroin is. Smokers have the chance to gradually discover the quality of the heroin they're taking by only lightly inhaling the first puff.

FIRST PERSON

CHARLIE FINLEY, HEROIN ADDICT

'I've never shot up. Needles scare me. But just chasing the dragon. Not in cigarettes. I liked to keep that separate, my fags for the pub, you know? It's what everyone was doing around this time. This was in 1985 or 1986, something like that. All the guys on our estate. There were hundreds of bits of foil or chocolate wrappers all over the walkways, under stairwells. Everyone was at it.

'I'd have a big roll of my mom's kitchen foil. I found some of the cheaper ones best because they were thicker and didn't bend all over the place. Sometimes I'd walk around with that inside my jacket all fucking day, tearing scraps off for myself or my mates. Otherwise it was a Kit Kat wrapper or the stuff they put inside fag packets, but that's thin and you needed to burn the paper off that so I preferred the foil.

'It's a case of what you know isn't it? I had a place I always went. It was like the smokers' room, a squat near where we lived. Someone lived there, but I never knew who it was. They'd always be a few of us in there smoking and I always thought that was a bit more sociable, you know? Rather than jacking up on your own and nodding out. We'd rig up a radio through some speakers and they'd be about three sofas all laid up against the walls, maybe a few cushions on the floor. But that was all the furniture. There wasn't really any upstairs, the roof was fucked and all the boards had gone. The only thing that worked in the kitchen was a gas stove. Someone had done the meter, so we had that on in the winter for a little heat.

'If someone was a little short maybe you'd help them out, 'til the next day. I never took much, though, so I didn't get tapped up much because if you're a junkie "the next day" never comes. You'd just smooth out the foil and heat it up a bit. Someone gave me a Zippo once, but I found that the flame was too fierce or I left it for too long under the foil. So I found the best lighters to heat it up were those pink or green disposable ones. Sometimes they'd burn your fingers and remind you to switch them off. They were also real cheap and you could also just flick them on and off quick. A bloke who had done some time showed me how to get an extra couple of days out of them when it looked like the gas had run out. But they are like 10p tops down the market so it weren't that big a deal.

'I'd grab a place on one of the sofas. You want somewhere comfortable. I'd see blokes around smoking standing up, but what's the point of that? Lay a bit of dope on my foil and get my tube ready. I've used everything for this. Plastic Bic pens, another piece of foil, rolled up, a straw, rolled up newspaper, a magazine. You name it. But then I found some thin tubing, which I cut down and used for years. I lined it with foil and every so often found I had a big enough deposit inside to give me another hit. It also stashed easily in my pocket and I liked the feel of it.

'I'd heat up the dope until it melts. It turns into a light brown oil. You can sometimes tell what sort of skag you've got then. If you leave the oil to set it should lift off the foil easily and be real hard. Sometimes you can see through it. But the best test is the taste. I noticed it's a bit different for everyone chasing the dragon. Some people I've seen heat everything up really quick and must lose a load of heroin because they can't suck it all in. I was always a bit more careful because when I did that myself I'd always burn my lungs with the smoke. So I kept the lighter flame real low and flicked it off so I think I got most of the heroin coming up.

'I could spend most of the morning in there, just with one £10 [$15] bag. I wasn't working then so there wasn't much else to do. I'd always take a couple of cans too. One to get me started. I'd leave the other for when I got back in the afternoon. Sometimes it was still there by the sofa, sometimes someone would have had a go at it.'

HEROIN SYRINGES

Syringes, needles. The works. Next to heroin itself, they are the most important part of the junkie's kit. Some junkies sleep with them. However, they can also be the weapon that finally kills them. Needles deliver the OD. They can also serve up HIV.

It's not always easy to spot the high-purity heroin that could lead to an OD, but at least infections and viruses can be avoided if syringes are used only once. Sometimes, this is not always possible. In the early years of heroin abuse, needles weren't readily available. The introduction of cheap works has helped solve this. Also, the user may not be able to access a ready supply of clean needles. He may be in jail, for example, and it is not unknown that one needle will serve the population of at least one prison wing. Sharing needles, spoons and filters has also, historically, been part of the junk experience. Long-time addicts sometimes pass on their knowledge – and works – to users when they fix them up and may become junkie buddies.

The threat of HIV in the early 1980s prompted action from governments and led to the introduction of pilot needle exchange schemes in the UK in 1986. These, which have been followed by similar schemes in many other countries, allowed users to swap their old works for a new, clean syringe. By 1987, 15 needle swap schemes were operating in UK cities such as Liverpool and Sheffield and, by 1991, some four million syringes were being distributed from around 200 swap agencies in the UK.

Misusers were targeted by locating near the user population in towns or by being mobile. The hours of opening were also fitted around the heroin users' clock – late to bed, late to rise – and evidence suggested that sharing diminished with the availability of clean equipment.

Needle exchanges are criticized by some politicians and pressure groups, who argue that they legitimize heroin consumption and also encourage the most dangerous method of administration. There are also complaints from the local population, worried that needle exchanges will draw heroin addicts to their neighbourhood and litter it with their dirty needles.

However, discarded syringes are usually already a problem in a neighbourhood before a needle exchange is set up. In the later 1990s there were numerous newspaper reports about children, refuse men and janitors accidentally jabbing – and sometimes infecting – themselves on dirty syringes, and exchanges often supply secure, plastic containers for safe disposal.

If syringes are shared, some users attempt to keep their works clean. Their methods are rudimentary, but give some measure of protection against infection. The safest way is to take the syringe apart and boil every part for at least ten minutes. However, not all syringes can take this punishment and drawing bleach or soapy water up through the needle is a more popular method; however, the cleaning fluid needs to be rinsed away thoroughly afterwards.

HEROIN ABUSE LEVELS

Heroin use is a global phenomenon – and problem. Of the 180 million people the United Nations estimates use an illegal drug, some 9.18 million around the world – or 0.22 per cent of the global population – were estimated to be heroin users in the late 1990s.

There are very few countries that heroin doesn't touch and infect with its attendant problems. This is demonstrated by the UN Office for Drug Control and Crime Prevention (ODCCP) *World Drug Report 2000*, which showed that of the 134 countries and territories surveyed, plant-based drugs such as the opiates, including heroin, were the most commonly abused. Some 76 per cent of those reported an abuse of heroin during the 1990s, significantly more than the 64 per cent and 24 per cent who reported cocaine and ecstasy abuse respectively.

> **Of the global population, 0.22 per cent were estimated to be heroin users in the late 1990s.**

The main regions of consumption are traditionally close to the areas of production and the large markets. Thus the highest rates of abuse of heroin are mostly concentrated in Asia (the highest levels of abuse are in Iran, Pakistan, India, and the Lao PDR) and Europe where 5.74 million and 1.5 million addicts respectively are believed to live.

WESTERN AND SOUTH ASIA

The highest rates of opiate abuse per capita of population are reported from the Islamic Republic of Iran, according to the UN ODCCP *Global Illicit Drug Trends 2000* report. This is mostly due to its proximity to Afghanistan, and estimates put the number of opiate abusers in the country at 1 million and, of those, there are some 400,000 heroin abusers.

The number of registered opiate users in India was 10,000 in 1999; however, this figure grossly underestimated the number of opiate users.

Official figures for those treated for opiate use show that the number of users rose from 27,000 in 1993/94 to around 40,000 in 1998, of which 21,500 were using mostly brown heroin. However, the UN's international Drug Control Programme (the UNDCP, part of the ODCCP) believes that some 3 million people are taking mostly opiate-based drugs in India, and around half of those could be taking heroin.

Raw opium is still the dominant drug in the states of Rajasthan and Punjab in the north, but heroin has overtaken opium as the main drug of choice in many areas in recent years. Brown opium, which is usually inhaled, is popular but in the state of Manipur, which borders Myanmar, the highly potent white heroin number four, which is normally injected, is more widespread.

SOUTHEAST ASIA

The number of officially registered drug users (mostly of opiates) in Myanmar was calculated at 86,000 in 1999, or around 0.2 per cent of the adult population. Around 31 per cent of these were heroin abusers and that proportion was expected to increase significantly as heroin gradually replaced opium as the traditional drug of choice. A 1998 survey in the Lao PDR revealed that more than 60,000 people were consuming opium. The number of registered opiate addicts in Vietnam in 1999 was 97,000, although the UNDCP estimates that the total number of drug addicts is closer to 185,000, or 0.4 per cent of the adult population.

A comprehensive 1993 survey in Thailand revealed that some 280,000 people abused opiates, of which 214,000 were taking heroin. There is also an upward trend in abuse in this country, which suffers from heavy opiate traffic from bordering Myanmar.

China experienced much growth in drug abuse rates during the 1990s. Estimates from the Chinese authorities put the number of registered drug users at 250,000 in 1993, but that figure more than doubled to 600,000 (approximately 80 per cent of these were heroin users) in 1998/99. However, some Chinese estimates put the number of addicts at between 2 to 3 million, which is 0.3 per cent of the population aged 15 years plus.

TABLE 2.3: EAST AND SOUTHEAST ASIA, MIDDLE EAST/SOUTHWEST ASIA, AND SOUTH ASIA – ANNUAL PREVALENCE OF OPIATE ABUSE AS A PERCENTAGE OF POPULATION AGED 5 YEARS AND ABOVE

EAST AND SOUTHEAST ASIA	%	YEAR
China	0.1	1998
Indonesia	0.01	1998
Japan	0.02	e
Lao PDR	2.1	late 1990s
Malaysia	0.2	1998
Myanmar	0.9	late 1990s
Singapore	0.3	1998
Taiwan	0.4	e
Thailand	0.6	late 1990s
Vietnam	0.4	1999
MIDDLE EAST/SOUTHWEST ASIA	**%**	**YEAR**
Bahrain	0.3	1998
Iran	2.8	1999
Israel	0.8	1995
Jordan	0.5	1998
Kuwait	0.01	1998
Lebanon	0.01	1998
Oman	0.01	1994
Pakistan	1.7	1999e
Qatar	0.01	1996
Syrian Arab Republic	0.02	1998
SOUTH ASIA	**%**	**YEAR**
Bangladesh	0.6	e
India	0.5	e
Maldives	0.9	1994
Nepal	0.3	1996
Sri Lanka	0.3	1997

(e = UNDCP estimate)
Source: UN ODCCP, *World Drug Report*, 2000

OCEANIA

In recent years Oceania, especially Australia, has reported increased heroin use with around 600,000 addicts estimated in the region. The 1998 Household Survey of Australia suggested that the number of heroin users was around 113,000 people, or 0.7 per cent of the population aged 15 or above. However, another 1997 survey estimated that there were 100,000 regular injectors with an additional 175,000 occasional injectors. In New Zealand a survey undertaken in 1998 showed that opiate abuse had reached approximately 0.6 per cent of the adult and youth population.

The annual UK consumption of pure heroin is estimated at between 28,000kg (25 tons) and 36,000kg (32½ tons).

TABLE 2.4: OCEANIA – ANNUAL PREVALENCE OF OPIATE ABUSE AS PERCENTAGE OF POPULATION AGED 5 YEARS AND ABOVE

OCEANIA	%	YEAR
Australia (14 and above)	0.7	1998
New Zealand	0.6	1998

Source: UN ODCCP, *World Drug Report*, 2000

WESTERN EUROPE

The number of opiate drug users in the European Union is somewhere between 1 million and 1.5 million people, with most of them using heroin. Abuse levels are the highest in Italy and the UK, where most drug agencies and government figures estimate that the number of heroin users is between 250,000 and 270,000. However, some experts, such as Release heroin project adviser Gary Sutton, say a more realistic figure for UK heroin users is between 300,000 and 400,000. Paul Hayes, chief executive of the National Treatment Agency (NTA), also expected the numbers to increase from 2003 as the NTA continued to roll out its programme to double the number of drug users in treatment by 2008. This would allow UK agencies to calculate a more comprehensive and accuratefigure for heroin users.

> The number of opiate drug users in the EU is between 1 million and 1.5 million people, with most of them using heroin.

A UK Home Office study carried out in September 2001 estimated that there were around 65,000 16 to 29 year olds taking heroin in England and Wales in 2000, although the higher estimate was put at the 113,000 limit.

In Austria, official figures in 1995 put the number of users of hard drugs at around 10,000, of which 4,000 were thought to be intravenous users. However, the AIDS service of Vienna suggests that the number of intravenous users is much higher, at around 25,000. In Belgium, official estimates put the number of addicts at somewhere between 15,000 and 20,000.

**TABLE 2.5: WESTERN EUROPE – ANNUAL PREVALENCE OF OPIATE ABUSE AS PERCENTAGE
OF POPULATION AGED 5 YEARS AND ABOVE**

WESTERN EUROPE	%	YEAR
Austria	0.2	1998
Belgium (18-65)	0.2	late 1990s
Denmark (18-69)	0.3	1995
Finland	0.05	1997e
France (18-69)	0.3	1997e
Germany (18-59)	0.2	1998
Greece (12-64)	0.4	e
Ireland	0.3	1997e
Italy	0.5	1997e
Liechtenstein	0.1	1998
Luxembourg	0.5	1997e
Malta	0.2	1998
Monaco	0.1	1995
Netherlands (12 and over)	0.2	1998
Norway	0.2	1994
Portugal	0.9	1998
San Marino	0.02	1997
Spain	0.6	1999
Sweden (15-75)	0.1	1997
Switzerland (18-45)	0.5	1998
Turkey	0.01	1998
UK	0.5	late 1990s

(e = UNDCP estimate)
Source: UN ODCCP, *World Drug Report*, 2000

CENTRAL AND EASTERN EUROPE

The largest market for opiates in Eastern Europe is the Russian
Federation, which had 350,000 registered drug – mostly opiate –
users in 1999 (up from just 131,000 in 1995). However, this was thought
to be only a fraction of the actual number of opiate users, with
some estimates rising to around 3 million. The UN puts the figure
closer to 1 million, or almost 1 per cent of the population. The most
popular drug in Belo-Russia is home-made heroin, produced from dried
poppy heads.

The ODCCP *Global Illicit Drug Trends 2000* report also showed that
Bulgaria and Croatia, which are along the main Balkan transit routes,
were reporting higher figures of heroin abuse. However, opiate abuse
appeared to have stabilized in the Czech Republic, where heroin is the
second most popular drug of choice after sedatives, and in Hungary,
where unofficial figures suggest that 100,000 people are on drugs such
as opium and heroin.

**TABLE 2.6: CENTRAL AND EASTERN EUROPE – ANNUAL PREVALENCE OF OPIATE ABUSE
AS PERCENTAGE OF POPULATION AGED 5 YEARS AND ABOVE**

CENTRAL AND EASTERN EUROPE	%	YEAR
Belarus	0.08	1998
Bulgaria	0.7	1998
Croatia	0.8	1997
Czech Republic	0.1	1997
Hungary	0.3	1999
Latvia	0.3	e
Lithuania	0.3	e
Macedonia	0.3	1998
Moldova, Republic	0.04	1997
Poland	0.3	e
Romania	0.03	e
Russian Federation	0.9	e
Slovakia (18 and over)	0.5	e
Slovenia	0.3	1993
Ukraine	0.3	1992

(e = UNDCP estimate)
Source: UN ODCCP, *World Drug Report*, 2000

THE UNITED STATES, CANADA, AND MEXICO

The USA is the next largest market for opiates after the EU. There were thought to be about 1.3 million hardcore heroin abusers in the late 1990s, although estimates vary. According to the 1998 National Household Survey on Drug Abuse, which may have underestimated illicit heroin use, an estimated 2.4 million people had used heroin at some time in their lives. Nearly 130,000 of them also reported using the drug within the month preceding the survey.

Although opiates account for around 24 per cent of all drug treatment demanded in the USA, 'heroin chic' in the mid-1990s and the availability of high-grade heroin on the market helped to boost user numbers in a country mainly known for cocaine abuse. A large proportion of these new users were smoking, snorting or sniffing heroin, and 87 per cent were aged under 26 years old. In 1992, only 61 per cent had been aged under 26.

The 1998 Drug Abuse Warning Network (DAWN), which collects data on drug-related hospital emergency department (ED) episodes, estimated that 14 per cent of all drug-related ED episodes involved heroin. More alarming was the fact that, between 1991 and 1996, heroin-related ED episodes more than doubled, from 35,898 to 73,846. Among youths aged 12 to 17 years old, the number of heroin-related episodes nearly quadrupled over the same period.

Emergency-room data shows that incidences of heroin abuse in the USA are particularly high in cities near trafficking ports such as Baltimore, New York, Boston, and Washington, DC, on the east coast; Chicago and Detroit around the Great Lakes; and San Francisco and Seattle on the west coast.

The Canadian authorities reported rising levels of heroin during the three years prior to 2000 as criminal gangs became more sophisticated in trafficking and the drug took hold amongst young urban users. Estimates suggest that some 0.2 per cent of the adult population

The number of US heroin users tripled in six years to over 200,000 in 1999.

consume opiates, with heroin abuse most prevalent in western Canada and the large cities of Toronto, Vancouver and Montreal where supplies are most freely available.

In Mexico, opiate abuse is put at more than 0.1 per cent of the population and the trend is upwards. Mexico is now not only the major transit point for drugs shipped into the United States, it has a growing demand problem of its own. While drug consumption in Mexico is still far below that of the United States, it began climbing in the mid-1990s at an alarming rate.

This increased drug use can be traced to a change in the practices of Mexican traffickers, who in the mid-1990s began to pay local employees, who fuelled their planes or drove their trucks, partly with drugs. In turn these people began selling drugs in their own home towns.

At the same time, the price of heroin has fallen. Drugs used to be beyond the means of the poor in border towns like Tijuana, but a shot of heroin now costs $5 (£3.50) to $10 (£7). Some Mexican law enforcement officials also report that the heroin problem has become worse since the 11 September terror attacks in New York because border security has sharply increased, making it harder for the cartels to move their heroin. They are consequently turning towards supplying their own youth.

SOUTH AMERICA

Overall opiate abuse in South America, Central America, and the Caribbean is not very high, with a total number of opiate abusers of less than 250,000. This approximates to under 0.1 per cent of the adult populations of most countries in these regions. The exceptions are Chile and Colombia, where opiate abuse penetration is running at levels nearer 0.3 per cent.

TABLE 2.7: CENTRAL, NORTH, AND SOUTH AMERICA – ANNUAL PREVALENCE OF OPIATE ABUSE AS PERCENTAGE OF POPULATION AGED 5 YEARS AND ABOVE

CENTRAL AMERICA	%	YEAR
Costa Rica	0.1	e
El Salvador	0.06	late 1990s
Honduras	0.1	1995
Panama	0.04	late 1990s
NORTH AMERICA	%	YEAR
Canada	0.2	e
Mexico	0.1	late 1990s
USA (12 and over)	0.5	1998
SOUTH AMERICA	%	YEAR
Argentina	0.03	1995
Bolivia (12–50)	0.04	late 1990s
Brazil	0.1	late 1990s
Chile (12–69)	0.3	1995
Colombia (12 and over)	0.3	e
Ecuador	0.4	1999
Venezuela	0.1	late 1990s

(e = UNDCP estimate)
Source: UN ODCCP, *World Drug Report*, 2000

AFRICA AND THE MIDDLE EAST

Despite major heroin-trafficking routes crossing some African countries, the overall level of opiate abuse here is quite low. However, the perception is that heroin abuse is rising in Morocco, Libya, Jordan, and Syria, which controls the Lebanon's Bekaa Valley, once a major producer of opium poppies and an area where small labs processed Southwest Asian opium.

Many Lebanese drug traffickers had professional and ideological links with the Palestinian Liberation Organization (the PLO) and many other armed Palestinian terrorist groups, including the Popular Front for the Liberation of Palestine and the Democratic Front for the Liberation of

Palestine. One major trafficker, Monser al-Kassar, effected heroin deals regularly exceeding 100kg (220lb) and was known at one time as the 'banker' of the PLO.

However, following pressure from the United States, the elimination of the Bekaa Valley poppy fields during the early 1990s appears to have had a major impact on heroin consumption, and no significant cultivation has been reported in this area recently. Syria is still considered to be one of the significant countries in the Middle East region for drug trafficking as it serves as a transit country for trafficking from Lebanon and Turkey.

TABLE 2.8: EAST AND SOUTHERN AFRICA, NORTH AND EAST AFRICA, AND WEST AND CENTRAL AFRICA – ANNUAL PREVALENCE OF OPIATE ABUSE AS PERCENTAGE OF POPULATION AGED 5 YEARS AND ABOVE

EAST AND SOUTHERN AFRICA	%	YEAR
Kenya	0.1	late 1990s
Namibia	0.1	1998
South Africa	0.1	1998
Zimbabwe	0.01	e
NORTH AND EASTERN AFRICA	%	YEAR
Ethiopia	0.04	late 1990s
Mauritius	0.8	1998
Morocco	0.2	late 1990s
Rwanda	0.04	late 1990s
Tanzania	0.02	1998
Uganda	0.04	late 1990s
WEST AND CENTRAL AFRICA	%	YEAR
Chad	0.2	1995
Ghana	0.7	1998
WEST AND CENTRAL AFRICA	%	YEAR
Nigeria (11–61)	0.3	late 1990s
Senegal	0.03	late 1990s
Sierra Leone	0.01	1997

(e = UNDCP estimate)
Source: UN ODCCP, World Drug Report, 2000

PROFILE OF A HEROIN USER

Who takes heroin? Junkies, sure. But how does one brother in a stable middle-class family take up the needle, while the other becomes a journalist on a national newspaper?

It's more complicated than sociology, genetics, and psychology can explain on their own, and clearly there are myriad reasons and influences that will persuade someone to use heroin. Environment, education, peer pressure, personality type, and ease of availability of heroin all play a part.

Studies show that certain people are more susceptible to using drugs – and subsequently becoming dependent on them – than others. There is no standard heroin-using profile. Users come from all socio-economic groups and from a wide range of personality types and family backgrounds.

However, studies have identified a series of risk and protective factors (see Table 2.9 below), which can work at various levels on the psychological development of an individual, and include the local or family environment, the personality of the user and education. Generally the greater potential for drug misuse and escalation to dependence and addiction depends on the balance of risk and protective factors.

For example, risk factors in the environment will include a high prevalence of drug taking among peer groups and easy availability of drugs such as heroin in the user's area. Again, a depressed, sensation-seeking personality will also predict a risk that could lead the individual to seek out a drug like heroin. Against this, someone with high self-esteem and an easy temperament is perceived as having in-built protection against turning to heroin or other drugs.

TABLE 2.9: RISK AND PROTECTIVE FACTORS

CLASS	RISK FACTORS	PROTECTIVE FACTORS
Environment	Heroin easily available Low household earnings Delinquent peers	Responsible peers High-earning household Good adult mentors
Family	Little parental monitoring Substance use by parents Divorce Unemployment	Tight-knit family Lots of parental supervision No history of drug use
Personality	Stress Depression Aggressive Impulsive, antisocial	High self-esteem Confidence Easy temperament
Education	Poor school performance Low aspirations High truancy rates	Good teacher relations High expectations Good qualifications

TABLE 2.9 CONTINUED

CLASS	RISK FACTORS	PROTECTIVE FACTORS
Other	Early deviant behaviour, including smoking, drinking Early sexual experiences Early use of other drugs	No deviant behaviour Religious involvement Negative expectations about substance abuse

Some attempt has also been made to create a picture of a typical heroin user, and a glimpse is provided by the 2001 study, *Drug Misuse Declared In 2000: Results From The British Crime Survey (BCS)*. This outlined drug use patterns among the population of England and Wales, and demonstrated that a young white man from Manchester with no academic qualifications is much more likely to become a junkie than a middle-class Pakistani women from a rural background, who went to university.

Some experts believe this UK study can be extrapolated to provide a basic profile of the features of drug and heroin users in Europe and many other western countries. *Drug Misuse Declared In 2000* showed that drug use was more prevalent among young people, with 50 per cent of 16 to 29 year olds reporting that they have tried drugs in their lifetime.

More specifically, those aged 20 to 24 years were the most likely group to have taken drugs in the last month or last year (of the study) and in their lives (see Table 2.10 below). Men were more likely than women to have used drugs. In the 20- to 24-year-old age group, 63 per cent of men compared to 54 per cent of woman had tried drugs in their lifetime – a ratio of 1.2 to 1. However, the gender gap widens as the experience of drug use grows shorter. For example, 1.4 more men took drugs 'in the last month' than women.

TABLE 2.10: DRUG USE IN LAST MONTH, YEAR AND LIFETIME

	16-19	20-24	25-29
Lifetime			
Men	44%	63%	60%
Women	40%	54%	40%
Last year			
Men	31%	34%	26%
Women	24%	26%	14%

TABLE 2.10 CONTINUED

Last month			
Men	21%	23%	19%
Women	12%	16%	6%

(e = UNDCP estimate)
Source: British Crime Survey 2000

The study also found that people tend to restrict their drug use to a single drug. In the last year, 15 per cent of 16 to 29 year olds used one drug, compared to 4 per cent who had used two drugs.

Use of opiates, including heroin, crack and methadone, was relatively low compared to drugs like cannabis, ecstasy, LSD, and magic mushrooms. Only 5 per cent of 16 to 59 year olds had tried opiates in their lifetime and, in the last year, only around 1 per cent of 16 to 29 year olds had taken heroin and crack.

The average age at which teenagers begin experimenting with heroin has fallen to only 15, two years younger than in the late 1980s, according to a Department of Health 2000 study.

The survey also suggested that drug use is not spread evenly around the UK and that certain drugs are more popular in different regions. London tends to have the highest rates of drug use, with over 30 per cent of 16 to 29 year olds reporting Class A drug use in the last year (of the study). That compared with about 20 per cent in Wales. However, in the same age group, use of heroin was highest in the north of England, the south and the Midlands with less than 0.5 per cent taking the drug in London and negligible usage in Wales.

The study also found that socio-economic factors - income level, education, type of neighbourhood - can contribute to drug usage and also influence the type of drug favoured. For instance, whereas cocaine use is relatively widespread across the whole population, heroin tends to be associated with less affluent groups. Very few 16 to 29 year olds from affluent urban, suburban, rural, or family areas reported using heroin in 2001.

This relationship between heroin and the less affluent was reinforced by measuring use of heroin with factors such as income, qualifications and employment status. The proportion who used heroin in the last year was found to be highest in the poorest households – those earning less than £5,000 ($7,300) – among those with zero academic qualifications, the unskilled and the unemployed.

According to a EU report on drug abuse, Ireland now has the youngest population of heroin addicts in Europe. Community workers battling the heroin crisis say they are coming across users as young as 12 and 13.

Heroin use in the UK has increased slightly since 1994 and the BCS 2000 survey showed that it is in the 16- to 29-year-old age group where the main increase has taken place. In 2000, 0.7 per cent of those surveyed in that age group said they had used heroin in the last year, compared to just 0.5 per cent in 1994 and 0.3 per cent in 1996.

The report shows that usage of the drug between genders has not shifted significantly over the years between 1994 and 2000, but rates of use of the drug in the last year for the unemployed were noticeably higher in 1998 and 2000 than for those in work.

Ethnic comparisons of drug use are also possible and the BCS 2000 survey found that, irrespective of age, white people were more likely to have taken drugs than black people, Indians or Pakistanis. Heroin, in particular, is almost unused in the UK among the latter two ethnic groups.

> 'Among the remedies which it has pleased Almighty God to give to man to relieve his sufferings, none is so universal and so efficacious as opium.'
>
> - Thomas Sydenham, English doctor, 1860

POPPY'S PROGRESS

Heroin is made from morphine, a naturally occurring substance found in the seed of the opium poppy. The history of heroin, therefore, starts with the opium. And this begins with the cultivation of the poppy, *Papaver somniferum*. The milky fluid extracted from the plant's ovary is highly narcotic after drying. This is opium, the name derived from the Greek word for 'juice of a plant'.

Around 3400 BC the first poppy was cultivated in lower Mesopotamia. Some archaeologists also claim to have found evidence of fossilized poppy seeds, which suggests that Neanderthal man may have used opium over 30,000 years ago. Excavations of the remains of Neolithic settlements in Switzerland have unearthed evidence that the poppy may have been cultivated then; perhaps for the food value in the poppy seeds.

The first reference to the poppy appears in a Sumerian text, which refers to it as Hul Gil, the joy plant, and the Sumerians soon passed on the art of poppy culling - and its euphoric effects - to the Assyrians. Some 2,000 years later, the Babylonians had introduced opium to the Egyptians, who began to cultivate fields around Thebes.

Priests encouraged the use of opium preparations for remedies, sometimes called thedacium after the potent Thebes poppy fields. A trade in opium soon flourished throughout the reigns of Thutmose IV,

Akhenaton, and King Tutankhamen with the Minoans and Phoenicians operating profitable routes across the Mediterranean into Greece and Europe. It also became common practice to entomb Pharaohs with opium artefacts.

In 460 BC the father of medicine, Hippocrates, acknowledged opium's use as a narcotic and styptic in treating internal diseases and, by AD 400, Alexander the Great had introduced opium to Persia and India, and Arabic traders were shipping the poppy to China.

Opium became a taboo subject during the Inquisition and it largely disappeared in Europe during the 14th and 15th centuries. However, by around 1500 the Portuguese had discovered that smoked opium produced instantaneous effects, and smoking the narcotic began to be the accepted method of taking the drug.

In 1527 opium was reintroduced into Europe through laudanum, a mix of alcohol and the drug, which was discovered by the Swiss physician Bombastus von Hohenheim. This gave successive generations, who added various spices to produce their own versions, access to mass sedation.

By the mid-17th century, opium had become the main commodity of British trade with China, its use thus taking root in the Far East. By 1839 it had also caused a war between the British and Chinese. The East India Company had enjoyed a monopoly on shipping opium from Bengal into China, and had rode roughshod over Chinese licences imposed to restrict imports of the drug by selling the drug to Indian merchants who smuggled it for them.

Despite the instigation of a House of Commons Committee of Enquiry in 1830, set up to investigate the company's opium dealings, the £2 million ($2.9 million) trade continued unabated, causing an epidemic of addicts among the Chinese population. At its highest point it was believed that there were around 15 million opium users.

In 1839 the Chinese government finally acted and confiscated some 20,000 chests of opium from British warehouses in Canton. In 1840 the British Foreign Secretary, Lord Palmerston, sent out a force of 16 British warships, which besieged Guangzhou and threatened communications with the capital.

This first Opium War was settled in 1841 with the Treaty of Nanking and China ceding Hong Kong to the British. The opium trade with China continued with new trading partners – the French and Americans – becoming involved in shipping the drug.

Some 15 years later Britain and China fought a second war when, in 1856, Chinese officials boarded and searched a British-flagged ship, the *Arrow*. The French joined the British in launching a military attack in 1857, at the end of which they demanded that the Chinese agree to the Treaty of Tianjin in 1858. This opened further ports to western trade and provided freedom of travel to European merchants inland. Trade in opium nearly doubled over the following two decades, but by this time China had also begun to grow its own poppy, which it traded in over the next century.

Many literary figures were also being seduced by opium, including John Keats, Shelley, Byron and Thomas De Quincey, who in 1821 published his autobiographical account of opium addiction, *Confessions Of An English Opium Eater*. And, in 1860, the English doctor Thomas Sydenham was moved to write, 'Among the remedies which it has pleased Almighty God to give to man to relieve his sufferings, none is so universal and so efficacious as opium.'

Opium is a complex chemical cocktail including sugars, proteins, fats, gums, ammonia and myriad alkaloids, notably morphine, codeine, noscapine, papaverine, and thebaine. Apart from thebaine, these alkaloids are used as analgesics and can reduce or abolish pain without loss of consciousness. However, it wasn't until 1805 that German scientist Friedrich Wilhelm Sertürner isolated the first alkaloid in its pure form from opium. Sertürner named the substance morphium (morphine) after Morpheus, the Greek god of dreams and sleep. It wasn't until a decade later that the powerful effects of morphine – the drug had at least ten times the potency of opium – were recognized and in 1821 a London pharmacist began producing it. Six years later German manufacturers E Merck & Company began the commercial production of morphine and in 1836 morphine entered the *London Pharmacopoeia*.

A new technique for administering the drug – and a crucial tool for today's junkie – arrived in 1843 when an Edinburgh-based physician Dr

Three Chinese men smoking opium. At the height of opium trading between Britain and China, there was an epidemic of addicts among the Chinese population. At its highest point, it was believed that there were around 15 million opium users.

An addict in the British Crown Colony of Hong Kong smokes from a homemade pipe made of an earthen jug and a bamboo stick.

Alexander Wood discovered the process of injection using a syringe. Injected morphine is up to 300 per cent more potent and, because the effect is almost instantaneous, it rapidly led to the intravenous use of the drug as a painkiller and for recreational use.

Opiate abuse in Europe and the USA had increased significantly by the mid-1800s. Opium dens, often run by Chinese immigrants, were opening in most American cities and even Old West towns where cowboys sat out herding duties laid up in dimly lit rooms smoking opium with prostitutes.

Opiate consumption in the USA also received a boost following the American Civil War in 1866. The wounded had been treated with morphine intravenously on the battlefield and, consequently, tens of thousands of soldiers became addicts. The medical establishment began to raise concerns about a new epidemic: morphine was being used by European and American doctors as a remedy to combat opium dependency and the addict would simply switch his addiction to morphine. Also, many patent medicines around at this time, such as laudanum and paregoric, contained opium extract. By the end of 1890s the United States was desperate to curb the non-medical use of opium.

Then a new drug was discovered, diacetylmorphine, or heroin. It was first synthesized from morphine by the English researcher CR Alder Wright in 1874 by boiling morphine with acetic anhydride over a stove. He was trying to isolate a powerful but non-addictive alternative to morphine. He failed. The white crystalline powder he discovered is between three and eight times more potent than morphine...and easily as addictive.

However, this wasn't realised at the time. In 1895 Heinrich Dreser, who was in charge of drug development at German drug manufacturers Bayer, began production of diacetylmorphine and coined the name 'heroin' after the German word for hero, *heroisch*.

Dreser tested the new synthetic drug on animals, human volunteers and himself, and declared it was an effective treatment for a range of respiratory ailments, including tuberculosis, asthma, coughs, emphysema, and bronchitis. He also declared that the drug was not habit-forming. In 1898, *The Lancet* introduced it to British physicians. It advised, 'heroin is said to be free from other disagreeable secondary effects of morphine'.

Commercial production of heroin began in 1898 and it was advertised by Bayer as a sedative for coughs rather than an analgesic. It was prescribed for a wider range of respiratory problems, such as whooping cough and hay fever. Doctors were also assured that its effects on motor skills and intellect were minimal.

Some dissenting voices warned of the dangers of addiction but, despite this, free samples of heroin were handed out to physicians. They often treated their patients' complaints with small doses of heroin administered orally via pills or pastilles, and drug companies manufactured over-the-counter drug kits containing a glass-barrelled hypodermic needle and vials of heroin. Bayer was soon selling heroin to dozens of countries, including the USA. The sales pitch was that it was a cure for morphine addiction: the modern heroin addict was born.

The income of the drug barons is an annual $500 billion (£345 billion), greater than the American defence budget.

However, by the early 1900s doctors began to notice that patients were consuming inordinate amounts of heroin-based cough remedies, and that heroin addiction in the UK and USA was out of control. Users – and the medical profession – soon realised that an addiction to heroin was more problematic than an addiction to morphine.

Heroin addiction in the USA became linked to legislative measures directed against illegal drugs and recreational usage such as the introduction of the Smoking Opium Exclusion Act 1909, which meant that American opium smokers found it difficult to find affordable opium. They switched almost exclusively to heroin, with heroin snorting soon becoming the popular method of administration.

During World War I, politicians and the media also whipped up a climate of hysteria against dope fiends enslaved by heroin. However, the arrival of the Harrison Act only managed to spread heroin use. Before 1914 most drug users remained loyal to one narcotic, but when new laws meant that their supplies of cocaine and other drugs were cut, they turned instead to cheap heroin. And once they had tried heroin, they stuck with it.

Heroin was finally outlawed in the USA in 1924. By that time, though, the market was already well established. There were too many addicts –

some estimates put the figure at 200,000 by the mid-1920s – for the health authorities to deal with. These addicts had already found ways to pay for their drugs and support their habit. They were turning to crime, principally stealing scrap or junk metal. Consequently, they became known as junkies – the name stuck.

FIRST PERSON

FULTON GILLESPIE, PARENT OF HEROIN VICTIM AND WITNESS AT A UK DRUGS INQUIRY BY A HOME AFFAIRS SELECT COMMITTEE, 2002

'I had been expecting Scott's death for some time. But when it came, just a month from his 34th birthday, it was none the less devastating. The blow was felt more keenly by his four siblings, especially his elder sister, Fiona, who was closest to him and who had tried so hard for so long to help him. But none of them, all drug-free, had suspected that he was so far down the road. The last time I saw him, just four days before he died, I knew he would not see 40 and said so. No one wanted to believe me.

'Up to his early teens, his school reports would have won him a place in heaven. He was everything any parent would have wished for – sensitive, conscientious, well fitted into school life and so on. Then a fellow pupil, a doctor's son, took some Valium tablets from his father's surgery and gave some to Scott. There was the wholly-to-be-expected flurry of panic-stricken letters between headmaster and parents, and the guilty boys were separated.

'But Scott had tasted the forbidden fruit and, for reasons he could never explain then or later, the taste and the danger appealed. None of the other lads involved ended up on drugs, only Scott. After another episode with pills when he was about 15, I sought advice from friends, doctors and psychiatrists. There was much hand-wringing but nothing else. Taking a stronger tack, I marched him off to Cambridge police station, where I had arranged for a chief inspector to receive us in full uniform. A stern lecture concluded with Scott being banged up in a cell for five minutes to give him a taste of what the future might hold. He was singularly unimpressed. It began to dawn on me that the son I once had, anxious to please, keen to play by the rules, was now rapidly slipping away. Why? What had we done? What made him different from the rest of the family? We didn't know then and we don't know now.

'At age 17 came his first arrest for possession of amphetamine sulphate. Stories in the local papers, family tears, public disgrace, embarrassment, humiliation for him, and more hunting around to find someone, some place, some service to help him. Nothing. A year later he was in court again on a similar charge, and this time he was found a place in a probation hostel. For a time, it looked as though he might find a new direction, but on his release he headed for London and we lost him for good.

'In the years up to his death, he kept in touch by letter and telephone, particularly with Fiona, and occasionally he would visit, or he and I would meet in a pub somewhere. His conversation was always about the pain of existence in a world where two-thirds starved so one-third could live well. He hated war, poverty and injustice, and felt powerless to alter things. But he would always try to get back home for the family Christmas, and we took heart from that, happy that he hadn't rejected us completely. On his last but one visit, I found him trying to steal from a handbag in the kitchen. I said nothing because his confusion and embarrassment said enough for both of us. I knew then, with total heartsink, that he was on heroin, because that's what heroin addicts have to do – steal from anyone or anywhere for cash to buy their stuff. This constant scraping around and the toxicity and the malnutrition is what eventually kills the addict. At his death, this tall, handsome, unaggressive misfit, who found the world so difficult to live in, had 29 convictions for theft, all to buy adulterated drugs.

By the summer of 1971, when United States involvement in the Vietnam War was near its peak, tens of thousands of American troops had become addicted to heroin.

'He spent the last five weeks before his death on remand for theft. He turned out to be innocent and was released. I picked him up and drove him to his flat. He was drawn and tired. He didn't want to come for a meal, he said, he just wanted to get his head down. My last words to him were: "Well, make sure you keep your head down." His parting words were: "Don't worry, dad. I'll be all right." Four days later he died, asleep in the arms of the old harlot, heroin.

'On the wall of his flat we found this hand-written valediction to the drug:

> *"The hot chills and cold sweats, the withdrawal pains,*
> *Can only be stopped by my little white grains.*
> *There's no other way and no need to look,*
> *For deep down inside you know you are hooked.*
> *You'll give up your morals, your conscience, your heart,*
> *And you will be mine until death us do part."*

'So why, in the wake of so much pain, do I want to see drugs legalized? Because I believe it was not the drug itself – unlike alcohol and tobacco, heroin has no known long-term side effects – but the criminalization of it that killed my son. In fact, a number of things contributed to his death: he was stupid enough to use heroin in the first place; he had spent five weeks in prison without drugs; on release his body could not take his normal dose (the coroner's view); and the heroin was toxic (revealed by the inquest pathology report).

'I am convinced that he would be alive today if all drugs had been legalized and controlled, because he would have had no need to steal and would not have been in prison, the heroin would have been controlled and therefore not toxic, and proper treatment would have been available under such a regulated system.

'Drugs, for me, should be a public-health rather than a criminal matter. First, they should be removed from the monopoly clutches of crime. Second, the billions saved in the costs of law enforcement, street crime and property theft should be redirected towards regulation, licensing, education, prevention, treatment and rehabilitation. The present uncontrolled drugs free-for-all will mean that thousands more will follow my son to the grave, victims of criminally supplied impure drugs, unless western governments recognize that the so-called "war against drugs" is unwinnable and wholly counterproductive.

'Many will ask how this can be morally justified. My view is that there is more moral justification in trying to cut crime and save lives than in leaving things as they are – under the control of criminals. Those who believe legalization will make more hard drugs available to more young people overlook the fact that drugs of all kinds are more available to more young people now than ever, even with prohibition in force. There is not a whit of evidence to support the idea that there is some massive reservoir of disaffected youth about to rush out and die. There are more pushers out there than chemists' shops, so those who want to use hard drugs are using them now and will continue to use them come what may. Therefore we should make sure the drugs they use are safe. This can only be done under legalized regulation.

'Just like alcohol prohibition in America, attempts at enforcement have served largely to demonstrate the lethal impotence of the law. We are beginning to see US-style gang warfare in our towns and cities. Apart from the health costs, multibillion-pound drug cartels, by bribery and terror, are undermining and corrupting law-enforcement and political systems across the world. Prohibition is simply fuelling this fire. We are spending billions dribbling water in at one end while criminals are making billions pouring their toxic fuel in at the other.

'Prohibition did not work in the past and it will not work in the future, simply because – now as in 1920s America – crime is controlling the supply. Therefore the link with crime must be broken. This would be a first step to removing the drugs issue from the monopoly control of crime and putting it where it belongs – in the area of public health, where it can be most effectively dealt with. Drug abusers, like alcoholics, should be treated as patients needing help rather than criminals to be punished. At present, we cannot control the drugs supply, either in quantity or quality, because we are not in charge of it. The Al Capones are.

'So we must dump prohibition and go for control by legalization. Setting up a royal commission would be a good start. Decriminalization will not provide a long-term answer because it leaves the offence on the statute book and leaves supply in the hands of crime. It will mean repealing or amending a number of United Nations treaties, including the 1961 UN Single

Convention on Narcotic Drugs, which prevents the unilateral legalization of hard drugs by individual governments. But the drugs laws provide governments with powerful enforcement tools which are often used for non-drug purposes – like Nixon and Watergate – so these are tools that will not be surrendered easily. Further, there are lots of people who live off drug prohibition who will not want to give up their seats at a number of influential tables.

'I am no advocate of drugs – I wish to God people wouldn't use them – because for my son the drugs road led to a very dead end. But that need not be so for thousands like him if we take control of the supply. At least we will be sure that they will get treatment and the chance of rehabilitation. And for those foolish enough to keep using, we will be sure that what they take will not kill them.'

'It's so good, don't even try it once.' - Anonymous heroin user

HEROIN PHYSIOLOGY

Heroin mimics the action of natural chemicals, called endorphins (endogenous morphines), which are produced in response to pain. They will act on specific opiate receptor sites in the brain and spinal cord to dampen the flow of nerve impulses in nerve tracts that carry pain information to the brain.

The opiate receptors - proteins embedded in the cell membrane - are not designed to recognize heroin, but are part of the human body's defence against pain and are normally activated by the endorphins. These chemicals are released in conditions of great stress and anxiety to 'cut off' pain, and explain why a soldier shot in battle may not immediately feel a wound or even realise that he has been hurt.

There are three different types of opiate receptor located in various parts of the human body and these will be activated by heroin entering the user's system. Those located in the brainstem are responsible for alerting the user to pain and one opiate receptor in particular - the mu-opioid receptor - is responsible for the pain-relieving and pleasurable effect of heroin. For example, if someone burns their finger on a hot saucepan, messages will be sent from the fingertips to the spinal cord, which telegraphs another message to the arm muscles to remove the hand - quickly. These are messages aimed at putting a direct stop to the painful stimuli.

However, to prevent the person from burning their fingers again, another signal is simultaneously sent from the spinal cord to the part of the opiate receptors in the brainstem, which will 'alarm' pain. However, the presence of opiates or heroin will remedy this through their analgesic effect. The feeling does not entirely disappear, but it loses its threatening character.

The critical aspect of heroin and other opiates is that this painkilling effect has little or no effect on other sensory perceptions such as motor functions and consciousness. This is very different from other non-opiate drugs, such as barbiturates, or substances like alcohol, which also have painkilling qualities, but will have a very significant effect on motor coordination, consciousness and intellectual capability. Although, at very high dosage levels, heroin can cause drowsiness.

Heroin does, however, have some major physical effects on other areas of the body. It can also have an effect on breathing because opiate receptors are also located in the respiratory centre. These are designed to regulate the frequency and beat of breathing, and allow steady inhalation depending on the level of exertion a person is experiencing. However, heroin will also have an inhibiting effect on these cells, often reducing the depth and frequency of someone's breathing. In the event of a heroin overdose, respiration will shut down completely. This will cause a shortage of oxygen to the brain and muscles and stop the heart.

Similarly, by influencing the hypothalmus, the area of the brain responsible for the hypophyis, controlling the body's hormonal balance, heroin can effect the levels of cortisol and testosterone in the blood and body temperature. This will decrease or increase slightly, depending on the dosage, but the effect may diminish through use and tolerance.

Opiate receptors can also cause vomiting. Normally stimulated by contaminated food, these cells are also pushed into activity by heroin, which explains why many first-time users throw up after a fix. Tolerance to this quickly builds, however, and it is unusual for regular users to vomit.

Heroin will also cause constipation because of the effect of opiates on the digestive system where many opiate receptors are also located. This is why opiates, which inhibit intestinal functioning, have been used as painkillers and for diarrhoea.

Another side effect of opiate use is that veins in the skin will be widened by the release of histamine. This has the result of giving the user a flushed and sweaty appearance, and it can also lead to constant itching.

The most visible and sometimes shocking side effect of heroin abuse is the effect on the pupils of the eye. They become like pin points, due to miosis (where the pupils contract) and this can happen almost immediately. This occurs even if the heroin user is fixing up in a darkened room, when the pupils are normally expected to become enlarged or dilated (mydriasis).

At the same time as creating euphoria by dampening distress, pain and other negative stimuli, heroin use can also lead to mood change. The opiate receptors in the limbic system can severely reduce the heroin user's appetite for sex. The signals to opiate receptors are not cut, but any cognitive link is leading to total emotional indifference.

Heroin is the fastest-acting of all opiates. Its increased liquid solubility allows it to cross the blood-brain barrier rapidly and the drug is reconverted back to morphine before it binds to the opiate receptors.

The effect of the drug is essentially the same regardless of the method of administration. However, when injected intravenously it reaches the brain in seven to eight seconds. This is the 'rush', an intense sensation following injection. Intramuscular injections, or skin popping, produce a relatively slow onset of this euphoric feeling, taking between five and eight minutes. The peak experience through smoking or snorting can take up to 15 minutes.

Users will offer a variety of responses to heroin, but there will always tend to be three effects associated with heroin use: those that are sought-after, such as euphoria and the removal of tension, and then the short-term and long-term side effects of taking the drug. These can range from nausea to malnutrition.

The surge of pleasure – the rush or buzz – seems to start in the abdomen. A warmth then spreads throughout the body and with this a dissipation of pain, fear, hunger, aggression, frustration, tension and anxiety. The user will feel calm. Time may seem to slow down, users may feel that they have a dry mouth and their limbs become heavy.

'I heard all this stuff about being in your mom's womb, you know like being in a warm place. Somewhere safe. Wrapped up in cotton wool, inside a big air bag. And they were right. That's exactly what heroin is.' – Kerry James, heroin user

The euphoria produced by heroin does not lead to a happy, smiling person. But it does remove the weight of the world from the user's shoulders. After the intense euphoria passes, users experience a period of tranquillity – sometimes referred to as 'being on the nod'. They will feel alternately drowsy and wakeful, warm and content, and may fall in and out of a sleeping state, often burning themselves or furniture if they are smoking a cigarette at the time. The narcotic power of the drug will diminish any feeling of pain if a user does injure him/herself. Mental functioning can become clouded due to the depression of the central nervous system. This feeling can last for up to an hour or more.

Experienced heroin users will inject between two and four times each day. After taking heroin, some people feel cocooned and emotionally self-contained. Others feel stimulated and sociable. Either way, there is a profound sense of control, and heroin also detaches the user from any feelings of pain or worry. They will also have slowed and slurred speech, a slow gait, constricted pupils, droopy eyelids and impaired night vision.

The euphoria gradually subsides into a dreamy and relaxed state of contentment. Higher doses of heroin normally make users very sleepy and very high doses will cause the user to slip into a semi-conscious state. The effects will wear off in three to five hours, again depending on the dosage.

HEROIN HEALTH

Heroin is not associated with good health. It's perceived as dirty and dangerous. Evil in a needle. In an ICM Research poll conducted for the UK's *Observer* newspaper in February and March 2002, 27 per cent believed that heroin was the drug likely to cause the greatest risk to health. Crack came in second at 19 per cent.

However, heroin has had a bad press. Unlike many narcotics, the drug is actually benign and there is little evidence to suggest that a lifetime of using pure dope would lead to anything more than a strong tolerance to the drug. This could lead to serious problems of dependency and withdrawal, but the real medical concerns that arise from chronic heroin use are due to other factors. These include adulterants in the dope, infected hypodermic syringes,

> **Heroin and morphine were implicated in 43 per cent of the 1,296 drug-related deaths during 2000 in England and Wales.**

the environment and habits of the addict, and methods of administration. Because the heroin abuser is always on the lookout for his next fix, he often neglects the normal necessary functions that people take for granted, such as eating and sleeping, and health problems set in through his general run-down condition. Spending any spare cash on drugs also means that his living conditions and diet are likely to be poor.

Initially, a new user will be recognized by their pale or jaundiced complexion and dramatic weight loss. The myriad complications associated with longer-term use include septicaemia, pulmonary abscesses and skin abscesses, and a long-term user may also find that the veins they use to inject become scarred or collapse, and will have to find new veins to inject.

Chronic users may also develop bacterial infection of the blood vessels, infection of the heart lining and valves, abscesses, cellulitis, and liver disease. Pulmonary complications, including a number of different types of pneumonia, may result from the poor health condition of the abuser as well as from heroin's depressing effects on respiration. Long-term physical effects can also result in respiratory system problems – breathlessness is a common complaint, as is coughing up phlegm – and chronic sedation.

Pure, unadulterated heroin does no damage to the body's organs. However, street heroin may have additives that do not really dissolve, and that result in clogging the blood vessels that lead to the lungs, liver, kidneys, or brain. This can cause infection or even the death of small patches of cells in vital organs. Immune reactions to contaminants can also cause arthritis and other rheumatologic problems.

Users also risk overdosing (OD'ing) because heroin is generally obtained from illegal suppliers and, therefore, the dose is unpredictable and may be dangerously adulterated by the dealer. An overdose (OD) will cause rapid heartbeat, heart failure, shortness of breath, ringing in the ears or head, pin-point pupils, clammy skin, convulsions, unconsciousness, and coma. When unconscious, users also risk the danger of choking on their own vomit.

Protracted use also causes extreme constipation and a loss of appetite. This can lead to malnutrition in addicts because they are never hungry and because the constipation can become so painful that they do not want to eat food.

Mental health problems can also result. Addiction and the psychological symptoms of withdrawal include depression, mood swings, and hypersensitivity to pain. The user will also lose their appetite for sex.

Abuse can also cause additional complications for women, whose livers are smaller than men's and will therefore be placed under more strain. Menstrual irregularity is likely and some women will cease ovulation. Pregnant drug users also risk miscarriage, stillbirth, or giving birth to smaller babies as a result of retarded growth in the womb or premature delivery. Congenital abnormalities are also common; they often exhibit a number of developmental problems and are at greater risk of cot death, or SIDS (Sudden Infant Death Syndrome).

Pregnant abusers can also cause irreparable damage if they suddenly withdraw from heroin, although it is very common that the baby will experience withdrawal symptoms after birth. Symptoms can vary enormously, but usually the baby will be hyperactive and restless. Sometimes the infant may even go into seizure, but often these effects can be minimized by a programme of tranquillizers such as chlorpromazine or benzodiazepine.

PHARMACOLOGICAL EFFECTS
DESIRED
- Warmth
- Sense of well-being and contentment
- Detachment from physical and emotion distress
- Relief from pain
- Reduced levels of tension and anxiety

SHORT TERM

■ Nausea
■ Vomiting
■ Drowsiness
■ Apathy and inability to concentrate
■ Constricted pupils
■ Death if respiratory depression caused by overdose

LONG TERM

■ Diminished appetite leading to weight loss and malnutrition
■ Constipation
■ Abscesses, if injected
■ HIV
■ Irregular periods
■ Physical and psychological dependence
■ Increased tolerance
■ Chronic sedation
■ Withdrawal symptoms, including sweating, chills, cramps, and diarrhoea

Potentially the most serious health risk to heroin addicts is that of contracting human immunodeficiency virus (HIV), hepatitis C and other infectious diseases through sharing and re-use of infected needles and injection paraphernalia. Drug abusers may also become infected through unprotected sexual contact with an infected person.

HIV is responsible for AIDS, and takes hold by attacking the immune system – the T-cells – of its host, which are normally responsible for fighting infection. HIV gradually destroys the ability of the immune system to mount a defence against other viruses or infections. Reported HIV incidence among those using heroin, and other injecting drug users (IDUs), is now a worldwide problem affecting countries from Australia to Argentina.

The UN Office for Drug Control and Crime Prevention report *Global Illicit Drug Trends 2000* stated that the practice of injecting heroin and other drugs was also spreading to developing countries and taking the

HIV virus with it. It blamed IDU as the major, if not the main, mode of transmission for HIV infection in North Africa, the Middle East, East Asia, Latin America, Eastern Europe, Central Asia, Western Europe, and North America. In the USA, it is thought that injection drug use has been a factor in an estimated one-third of all HIV and more than half of all hepatitis C cases.

In 1999 the steepest HIV curve was found in the former states of the Soviet Union. The virus is understood to have spread from the Ukraine in the mid-1990s to the Baltic states, the Caucasus and Central Asia where IDU is perceived as the primary cause of HIV. In Moscow alone, in 1999, 2,700 new HIV cases were reported, three times as many as in all previous years combined; a high proportion of these were blamed on heroin users fixing up.

Other Central and Eastern European countries believed by the report to be at risk from the HIV epidemic spread by IDUs are the Czech Republic, and Serbia and Montenegro in the Balkans.

Drug injection – and HIV – was also believed to be on the increase in China and Myanmar, where it is understood to be diffusing from urban to rural areas. Heroin injection, already established in Hong Kong and Thailand, was also reported to be spreading to Vietnam and Lao PDR. In 1995 it was estimated that 77 per cent of HIV infections in Malaysia were among IDUs.

> Between 1987 and 1997, there was a ten-fold increase in the seizure of illicit drugs, and yet the supply on the streets was so strong that the price of these drugs had kept dropping.

In Australia, heroin is the most commonly injected drug and HIV prevalence among IDUs is less than 5 per cent. The number of people with HIV in Austria is thought to be between 12,000 and 14,000, nearly half of whom are drug users. HIV infection in Austria among drug users varies from around 12–30 per cent in Vienna to 50 per cent in western parts of the country.

In the UK, the spread of HIV among heroin users and other IDUs has been largely stopped due to the success of the mid-1980s decision to implement a policy of clean needles. By March 1999 almost 3,500 drug injectors had tested positive for HIV, and more than 1,000 had been diagnosed with AIDS. However, drug researchers believe this has abated.

Research has also discovered that drug abusers can change their risk-taking behaviour – sharing syringes, unsafe sexual practices and so on – through drug abuse treatment, prevention, and community-based outreach programmes.

Sharing needles also puts the heroin user at risk of hepatitis, a viral infection that attacks the liver and that has affected the drug-injecting community for longer than HIV. There are three stains of hepatitis:

- **Hepatitis A** – Associated with poor hygiene, and spread through water and food contamination
- **Hepatitis B and C** – Most relevant to injectors.

Hepatitis B is transmitted through blood, but can also be passed though saliva and semen. It incubates for around three months before exhibiting a range of flu-like symptoms. The virus will clear up and a full recovery is normally expected in around six months.

Hepatitis C (HCV) is probably the most serious form of hepatitis and, unlike hepatitis A, can lead to chronic liver damage in 70 per cent of sufferers, and sometimes death. It is estimated to have infected around 35,000 people in the UK alone and although it is impossible to put a figure on the number of those infected through heroin use, it is likely to be in the low thousands. The disease kills about 8,000 people annually in the USA, and about 3.9 million Americans are believed to be infected with the virus. By 2010 it is estimated that up to 39,000 people in the USA will die from the disease each year.

However, it is not necessary for the heroin addict to have shared a needle with a hepatitis C sufferer. The National Center for Infectious Diseases warns that the sharing of *any* drug equipment, such as razors or mirrors, can potentially be harmful.

What makes the virus particularly difficult to diagnose is that around 80 per cent of those with hepatitis C do not display any symptoms. Those that do will experience flu-like aches, fatigue, jaundice, diarrhoea, abdominal pain, and loss of appetite. Around one-fifth of sufferers will clear the virus trom their systems in up to 12 months, but in others the disease can remain dormant for anything up to 30 years and by that time irreversible liver damage may have been done.

> *'I think I got it [hepatitis C] from dirty needles in the 1980s and it means I've had to give up any hard drinking. I can just about manage a pint of cider every so often, but that's against doctor's advice. Hepatitis has really fucked me up physically.'*
>
> − Lee M, heroin addict with hepatitis C

It is estimated that some 40 per cent of hepatitis C patients can be successfully treated with recent advances in medication administered for the disease. Alpha interferon (IFN-alpha) alone, or in combination with oral ribavirin, is commonly used and combination therapy (interferon plus ribavirin) is rapidly superseding interferon monotherapy because this dual therapy is significantly more effective.

The standard interferon regimen for patients with chronic hepatitis C consists of three IFN-alpha injections per week for up to 18 months. Some 40 per cent of patients treated with IFN-alpha alone can retain normalized liver function.

Treatment with interferon leads to a variety of side effects, which can significantly impair quality of life. Some clinical trials suggest that over 60 per cent of patients treated with IFN have influenza-like symptoms. Other common and disabling side effects are chronic fatigue and depression.

Treatment with IFN and ribavirin is effective in clearing HCV in almost 40 per cent of treated patients, however combination therapy is expensive and carries significant side effects, particularly anaemia, depression and weight loss.

The ultimate price to pay for using heroin is death. Many heroin deaths are through suffocation, usually if the user's air passages are blocked by vomit and they have fallen asleep or slipped into unconsciousness.

Overdose of heroin − OD, or dropping − when the body hasn't built enough tolerance to cope with the quantity of the heroin taken, is another frequent danger. Overdose is very common and even small amounts of heroin may cause some people to OD after a period of non-use. This often happens if an addict has been in prison or hospital, and when they return to heroin and pump their normal dose into a vein, the body can't cope. Sometimes junkies can simply take too much, perhaps because they have a supply from a new source, or the heroin they score could be significantly purer than the cut dope they regularly inject.

PHYSICAL SYMPTOMS OF HEROIN OD

- Abnormal or very slow breathing
- Cold skin and low body temperature
- Slow heartbeat
- Muscle twitching
- Slow working of the central nervous system
- Gurgling sound in the throat from vomit or saliva
- Blue tips of fingernails and toenails because of low oxygen
- Small pupils
- Drowsiness
- Unconsciousness
- Coma

An OD victim may go into a coma or die. OD death – or in junkie argot, pulling a blue one or bluey – can take the form of heart failure, liver failure or respiratory failure, and the physical symptoms of a fatal heroin dose will start with slow, shallow breathing and the pupils will turn to pin points. Blood pressure will drop alarmingly, the skin will turn blue and the OD victim will slip into unconsciousness and coma. Death can be almost immediate or the whole process can take up to ten hours.

The best way of preventing overdose is to not use heroin alone, and many users have buddies to fix up with. Neither should heroin be used in tandem with alcohol, tranquillizers or other drugs, and if the drug has been bought from a new dealer, a small amount should be tried first to test how pure the heroin is. Antagonists, which block the action of opioids such as naloxone, can also sometimes reverse the effects of OD.

OD DOS AND DON'TS

DO

■ phone an ambulance immediately and tell the operator that the person has overdosed

■ stay with the OD victim

■ keep the OD victim awake by walking them around and talking to them

■ if the OD victim is unconscious, put him or her in the recovery position

■ check his or her breathing and clear their airway

■ administer mouth-to-mouth resuscitation if he or she stops breathing

DON'T

■ inject the person with any other drug

■ put him or her under the shower

■ put anything in his or her mouth

Real problems can also result if the injector hits an artery (arteries take blood away from the heart, whereas veins return the blood to the heart). Sometimes the plunger in the syringe will be forced back by the high pressure of the blood and rapid bleeding will result; this will need urgent attention, otherwise it can result in the loss of limbs and sometimes death.

It is almost impossible to get accurate statistics on heroin-related deaths, because the definition of heroin-related deaths is potentially very wide. It could, for example, include accidental overdose, suicides through overdose, poisoned heroin, accidental death while under the influence of heroin, death from AIDS after contracting the HIV virus through injecting heroin, and murder or manslaughter while under the influence of heroin.

Often, doctors will record the cause of death without making any mention of the drug in the system. However, the UK's Office for National Statistics (ONS) has estimated the number of drug-related deaths for England and Wales (see Table 4.1), which include accidental and deliberate narcotic overdose (excluding paracetamol). In 1993 there were about 900 deaths caused through drug abuse, rising to just over 1,700 in 1997. Of these, 255 were directly related to heroin and another 421 were linked with methadone, commonly used by heroin addicts to break their dependence. Just 38 deaths were caused by cocaine and there were 12 through ecstasy use.

Further research implicated heroin and morphine in 43 per cent of the 1,296 drug-related deaths during 2000 in England and Wales, which suggested that the number of heroin deaths had risen by one-third to 551. Many of the heroin-related deaths were caused because users had taken a cocktail of drugs, and the statistics appear to show that 'most at risk' is the heroin addict.

TABLE 4.1: DRUG-RELATED DEATHS

DRUG TYPE	NUMBER OF DEATHS
Methadone	421
Heroin	255
Temazepam	104
Amphetamines	40
Cocaine	38
Ecstasy	12

Source: Office for National Statistics, 1997

Around the world, heroin deaths also appear to be on the increase. In Australia there were just six in 1964 compared to 600 in 1997. Austria reported 86 drug-related deaths in 1988 and Belgium had 91 drug deaths in 1990, most through heroin abuse.

FIRST PERSON
JOHN LLEWELYN, FORMER HEROIN ADDICT AND DEALER TURNED HEROIN COUNSELLOR

'The seeds of my drug-taking career were sown when I was 12 and I discovered alcohol. I was an army cadet and I customized my uniform to look like a regular soldier's, which added on a few years. I used to march into pubs, bold as you like, and order a drink. No one questioned me and I could indulge to my heart's content.

Heroin user preparing the drug before injecting. The white powder is prepared for use by being mixed with water and heating in a spoon before injection. The drug induces stupor and narcotic sleep states in users, while long-term use causes dependence and tolerance, leading to ever-increasing doses being taken, often resulting in fatal overdoses. Addicts who try to stop using the drug suffer from range of withdrawal symptoms, including muscle spasms, cramps, and psychological problems.

Heroin addict shooting up. The strap wrapped around his upper arm makes the veins swell up, making the injection easier to perform.

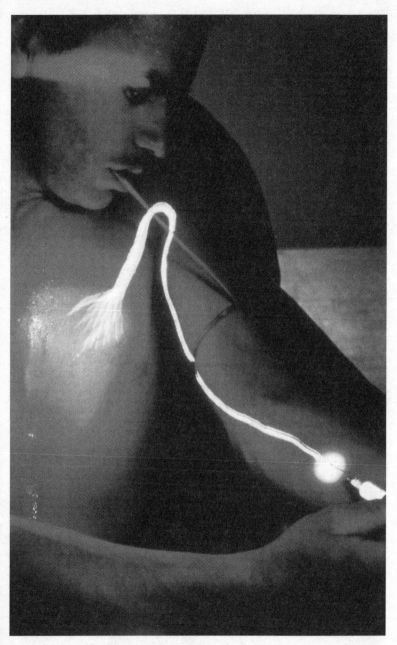

The path of the injected drug through the vein towards the heart. Heroin is widely used as a recreational drug for the psychological 'high' it induces, despite laws prohibiting its use and the dangers of side effects, including addiction, constipation, drowsiness, and respiratory depression.

'In the early 1960s when I was about 14 I got into marijuana. But what I will say 40 years on is that marijuana never led me into taking hard drugs. The so-called experts like to call marijuana a gateway drug, but it didn't get me on to heroin, I can tell you that, and 90 out of 100 users will tell you the same thing. I was always keen to try everything that was going. I was curious. I tried uppers and downers, purple hearts.

'At 18 I joined the regular army and was based at Lichfield. It really was the good life. Everything was ahead of me. I was drinking a lot at this point. I was 18 and my days were a blast. I was a real jack-the-lad. I smoked heroin for the first time with a group of army pals. From the first puff I loved it. I felt I was floating out of this world and into another. I thought it was the bee's knees. I certainly didn't see any harm in it.

'At this point I was married but my wife died very suddenly and unexpectedly. Her death was the perfect excuse for me to overindulge in everything and anything, and I went completely off the rails. I was given 12 months' leave, my children were adopted by my sister-in-law and I spent that year drinking and smoking heroin.

Between 1990 and 1995, heroin-related deaths in the USA increased by 134 per cent from 1,976 to 4,625.

'In 1966 I was discharged from the army and given a tidy lump sum, which I spent buying a nightclub in Liverpool. All the threads holding me together started to unravel. I got friendly with the notorious Richardson gang, I changed my name, I started robbing banks. I got mixed up in all sorts of things. Looking back, I don't know how it all happened. I guess the drink and the drugs convinced me that I could do anything, be anyone I wanted. I was living the high life – it was all fancy restaurants, nightclubs, gambling, glamour.

'Between 1967 and 1978 I started importing drugs. I dealt mainly in heroin, cocaine, and amphetamines. The drugs would come through France and Spain by boat, and the pick-up point was Padstow in Cornwall. I'd bung a couple of local fishermen £500 [$725] and they'd go out and pick up the gear. I used to pick up a hundredweight of stuff at a time.

'There was something really thrilling about watching the boat set off in the middle of the night and then waiting for it to come back with my catch of the day. I was never caught, though I don't know how I got away with it. I was a wholesaler and would pass it on to dealers. I was getting it at 100 per cent pure and I'd put it out at 60 per cent. I never had any qualms about what I was doing. If people wanted it why not? I was providing a service.

'But then I started sampling my own wares. Big mistake. I turned into a real nasty shit. It was such good stuff that I couldn't keep my hands off. I was like a kid with a sweetie jar. I kept telling myself "just once more" but I couldn't stop. I was still smoking the heroin, not injecting at this point. I opened another nightclub in Manchester. I did a bit of car dealing. I got into pimping for a while. I really was the lowest of the low. My life was devoted to drugs and making money.

'In 1969 I jacked up for the first time. That first experience is still as vivid today as it was at the time. The procedure is so involved and the rituals combine to heighten that feeling of intense anticipation. First, there's cooking the drug over a candle, then drawing it into the needle. The instant you know you're within seconds of taking heroin, all anxiety seems to evaporate. You flush the needle to get rid of the air bubbles and then slowly, gently, push the needle in.

'It's part pleasure, part pain. The rush is instant. Within a few seconds everything calms down. Total peace. You get a warm feeling right through your body. Warm, comfy, safe. Then you start to nod. Bliss. The first time I jacked up, that feeling lasted for an hour, the second time 40 minutes, the third time 20 minutes. Within two months it was down to five minutes. Addiction is threefold – it's mental, physical and spiritual.

'After this point heroin began to dominate my life. I was 24 and the next five years were totally, totally mixed up. I was still importing drugs, I took on another gang and got shot. Some friends smuggled me out to a hospital in the Canaries where I could recover without arousing suspicion. Everything began spiralling out of control. One minute up, the next way down. Friends kept telling me "if you use, you lose", but I wouldn't listen. I thought I was invincible.

'The turning point came in 1978. I'd just done a deal. I had £40,000 [$58,000] in the back of a Mk II Jag and I was driving through Wolverhampton on my way to Preston. I don't know what hit me but I got an urge to pull off the motorway. I left £30,000 [$43,500] in the car, took £10,000 [$14,500] with me and went on a bender in Liverpool. To this day I can't remember what happened. All I know is that I ended up with two prostitutes who saved my life. They were the ones who got me off heroin for good. They must have looked at the state of me and come to the conclusion that I wasn't going to be around for much longer if I carried on using.

'They locked me in a room and got me off heroin. Cold turkey style. It was horrendous. It's like having pins and needles but 100 times worse, from your scalp to the tips of your fingers. At times the pins and needles would get worse, like a Chinese burn when someone twists really, really hard. I was hallucinating and shaking like a skeleton in a biscuit tin. I felt sick. This was going on 24 hours a day. I survived on vodka and dry Sugar Puffs. The two girls screwed me rotten to take my mind off what was going on. I was a disgusting piece of humankind. Shitting myself, screaming for a fix. I don't know what reserves of strength I managed to call on, but after a couple of days I knew I was going to get through it.

'In the meantime the police had found my car and were looking for a body. I knew I couldn't go back to that world. If I did, I'd just sink straight back into it. For the next couple of years I lived on the streets. It wasn't the high-rolling life I'd been used to, but at least I was drug free. In 1980 a lady took pity on me in Kidderminster. I don't know what made her connect with me but she saw something, some way of saving me. She took me home with her and I had a bath. I dunno, maybe I didn't look too bad when I cleaned up because she decided to keep me. We had 16 years and two children together. I got sober and to this day I haven't used anything since. What I will say is that alcohol did more damage to me than all the drugs I took. Alcohol is the thing that screws up your mind and your liver, and yet it's legal.

'In 1991 I set up my first drug rehabilitation home in north Devon. I'm not a religious man but I'm spiritual and I had an overwhelming compulsion to do some good. It's a cliché but I felt it was time to put something back. I borrowed the money from old contacts. The first place was trial and error. I didn't have a clue what I was doing, but I had enough personal experience as a dealer and a user to get into a heroin user's mind-set. Today I've got three drug rehabilitation homes. I'm dealing with magistrates and judges and the police on a daily basis, and over the last few years I've found out everything there is to know about the drug laws in this country.

'Ninety-nine per cent of the heroin users who come to us have been in trouble with the law. The heroin problem is getting out of hand. In the beginning, 95 per cent of the people who came to us had a problem with alcohol, 5 per cent with drugs. Now it's 70 per cent drug related and 30 per cent alcohol. Of those who have a drug problem, the vast majority are on heroin. Young people have the attitude that they can handle heroin: "I don't have a problem. I'm not dependent", that sort of thing. How wrong they are. I've been there myself and I know how you can convince yourself of anything when your mind is floating six feet in the air.

'The government doesn't know how to treat people with addictive natures – it treats the symptoms but not the problems – why people start using heroin in the first place. At my homes we practise non-confrontational therapy. Central to my way of working is trust. I trust all the people who come to us. For example, I'll take a user who is a thief and give them money to go shopping. They won't have experienced that level of trust before. Society regards them as dirty junkies but I give them back their self-respect.

'We take people in and let them recover in their own time. They get three meals a day, a warm bed and we let them talk when they're ready. There's no pressure. Their friends and families have usually given up on them and we pick up the pieces. I would say that 80 per cent of the people who come to us clean up and return to their families. We don't set any time limits. We'll support them for as long as it takes. It could take years but as far as I'm concerned that doesn't matter. It doesn't matter if they fail. The key is to keep trying. I've got one gentlemen with me at the moment who's been with me for seven years. He's 63 now but he's determined to get off heroin. I'm not interested in statistics, how many people I can get off heroin in a year, I see these people as individuals. The key is not just to get them off heroin but to keep them off.

'I still have the urge myself. I'm 54 now and it's been 21 years since I had a drink or touched drugs. In the early days the urge to score would last for hours, these days it lasts for minutes but it's still there. Sometimes I look at the people who come to us for treatment and I think, you really don't know the half of it. "If you want to know what it's really like to be at the absolute bottom of the heap with your life in shreds, sit down for a couple of hours and I'll tell you a story." Sometimes they listen, sometimes they don't. But the fact is I'm clean and I'm still alive and they can't argue with that.'

HEROIN ADDICTION

Addiction or dependence means that a large part of a person's life is governed by drugs. Buying them and taking them. It is a chronic, relapsing disease, characterized by compulsive drug seeking and use, and by neurochemical and molecular changes in the brain.

And it's a growing problem. Dependence – a strong compulsion to keep taking drugs – is an insidious aspect of any recreational abuse. UK charity group Action on Addiction estimates that around one in three adults in the UK suffers from some form of addiction, costing the tax payer around £5 billion ($7.25 billion) in 2002.

Not all drugs are as addictive as others. Many drugs users can drink alcohol and then not touch a drop of the hard stuff for months. And US research, available through the American National Comorbidity Survey, demonstrates that cannabis has a very low potential for dependence.

Heroin is a different matter. Heroin produces profound degrees of tolerance and physical dependence, which are also powerful motivating factors for compulsive use and abuse. As with abusers of any addictive drug, heroin abusers gradually spend more and more time and energy obtaining and using the drug. Once they are addicted, the heroin abusers' brain becomes wired to that drug and their primary purpose in life is to seek out and use more and more heroin. (Physical dependence is not inevitable, however, and some heroin users are able to take it on an occasional basis.)

Although heroin is not used as widely as many other drugs, such as tobacco or alcohol, once tried, a very high proportion of users will go on to use it regularly; they will become totally dependent on it. They will be addicted, and dependence is one of the main characteristics that pervades heroin use and informs treatment for the drug.

One symptom of heroin is physical dependence, which does not occur with ecstasy, LSD or softer drugs like cannabis. This results from repeated, heavy use of the drug and can alter the body chemistry, building up tolerance to the drug. The body adapts to the presence of the drug and withdrawal symptoms occur if use is reduced abruptly. Withdrawal may occur within a few hours after the last time the drug is taken. With regular heroin use, tolerance develops. This means the user must use more and more heroin to achieve the same intensity or effect.

Withdrawal symptoms will occur if use is reduced or stopped. Withdrawal begins between 8 and 24 hours after the last fix and the symptoms are muscle aches, diarrhoea, cold flushes, goose bumps (cold turkey) and tremors, sweating, chills, runny nose, nausea, insomnia, muscular spasms, kicking movements ('kicking the habit'), yawning and sneezing. Elevation in

'Drug addiction is a state of periodic or chronic intoxication, detrimental to the individual and to society.' UN Commission on Narcotics definition

blood pressure, pulse, respiratory rate and temperature occurs as withdrawal progresses. These effects will fade after a week to ten days, but a feeling of weakness may persist for several months after quitting the drug.

Major withdrawal symptoms peak between 24 and 48 hours after the last dose of heroin and subside after about a week. However, some people have shown persistent withdrawal signs for many months. Heroin withdrawal is never fatal to otherwise healthy adults, but it can cause death to the foetus of a pregnant addict.

Tolerance develops to the respiratory depressant, sedative, analgesic, emetic and euphorigenic effect through heroin use, so addicts will need to inject increased dosages to achieve the same effect they did weeks, months or years before, and if they terminate use they will suffer withdrawal effects. Sometimes addicted individuals will endure many of the withdrawal symptoms to reduce their tolerance for the drug so that they can again experience the initial rush.

Craving and relapse can occur weeks and months after withdrawal symptoms are long gone. Patients with chronic pain who need opiates to function (sometimes over extended periods) have few if any problems leaving opiates after their pain is resolved by other means. This may be because the patient is simply seeking relief of pain and not the rush sought by the addict.

At the same time, the heroin addict will also evolve a psychological dependency, which is more common with users of other drugs. Essentially, this means the person using the drug feels they are unable to cope with the world unless they are under the influence of heroin, and friends, family and activities such as work take a secondary role.

Heroin dependency will often include both physical and psychological factors, and this has helped to produce more accurate definitions of drug dependence. Historically they have been framed in pejorative terms because early thinking tended to perceive addiction as simply a physical concept – a vice. More recently, psychological dependence has played a greater role. An expert committee working for the UN Commission on Narcotics in the early 1950s stated that addiction characteristics included an 'overpowering desire or need to continue taking the drug and to obtain it by any means; a tendency to increase the dose; a psychological and sometimes a physical dependence on the effects'. This differs markedly from a description of a habit-forming drug, which is generally understood to mean a narcotic that can be taken repeatedly without creating the bonds evident in addiction and that doesn't adversely affect the user.

> 'I'm hooked on both man. Crack is impossible, you get me? I can do six, seven rocks a day easy then leave it alone for a week, especially if I ain't got the cash. But heroin. That got me good. It ain't possible to break free. I know, I tried dozens of times. Impossible. It's heroin though man, that's what it does.'
>
> Jenny T, heroin and crack addict

In her 1999 account of her own experiences with the drug, *How To Stop Time: Heroin From A To Z*, Ann Marlowe attempts to explain her dependence to addicts as being similar to the satisfaction they will experience with their first coffee of the day. Subsequent coffees will never be the same. Marlowe wrote, 'The chemistry of the drug is ruthless: it is designed to disappoint you. Yes, once in a while there's a night when you get exactly where you're trying to go. Magic. Then you chase that memory for a month', adding that her definition of heroin addiction would be 'a form of mourning for the irrecoverable glories of the first time'.

The intensity of the intravenous high created through heroin means it is very likely that recreational use of the drug will lead to physical addiction and dependence. Heroin's ability to create dependence is neatly summed up in Table 4.2, which shows the use of six drugs by a US sample group and the proportion of those who developed a dependence. Alcohol was the most commonly used, with 91.5 per cent of the US

The cost of addiction to the British tax payer is £5 billion ($7.25 billion) per year.

Household Survey admitting its use. However, transition from use to dependence for alcohol was relatively low with only 14.1 per cent developing an addiction.

At the other end of the scale, only 1.5 per cent of those surveyed had tried heroin, but of those 0.4 per cent developed an addiction. Thus, almost a quarter of those who do try the drug will end up with an addiction. That compares with less than one in ten of people who develop an addiction to cannabis, despite it having been tried by approximately 30 times more people.

	TABLE 4.2: DEPENDENCE		
Drug	Proportion of population who have used	Proportion who have developed dependence	Proportion of dependence
Tobacco	75.6%	24.1%	31.9%
Heroin	1.5%	0.4%	23.1%
Cocaine	16.2	2.7%	16.7%
Alcohol	91.5%	14.1%	15.4%
Cannabis	46.3%	4.2%	9.1%

Source: US Household Survey

HEROIN PREVENTION

Preventing people from becoming heroin addicts in the first place is an objective of all governments attempting to contain their drug problems.

If they are successful at stopping new users adopting heroin, their countries' injecting and smoking population will gradually reduce to zero.

Unfortunately, most drug experts concede that until prevention models become more complex to match the social factors being brought to bear on a heroin user, they will have only moderate success. History seems to support this view because prevention methods have had little or no effect at stopping the growth of the world's heroin problem.

DRUG PREVENTION AND EDUCATION

- Drug education has limited effect on behaviour and is unlikely to prevent teenagers from experimenting with drugs
- Education can increase knowledge, but strategies need to be based on a range of consistent approaches
- Education can contribute towards increased safety
- Shock tactics are generally believed to be counter-productive
- Measuring the effectiveness of drug prevention programmes is very difficult
- Prevention is neither a cheap nor easy option

Drug prevention is about raising knowledge and awareness which, given enough resources, are achievable objectives. However, in tandem with increasing information about heroin is the objective to change behaviour. Harry Shapiro communications director at UK drug resource DrugScope says this is the hard part: 'It is very difficult to do. How can you get people to change their habits? There is a very rapid decay factor with information campaigns, a couple of weeks later people forget all about it.' However, Shapiro believes that the messages can sometimes sink in over time in the way that 'it has now become a lot less fashionable to drink and drive'.

'As drug prevention enters its fifth decade we still have no definitive answer to the question "What works?"'. David Best and John Witton at the National Addiction Centre

What is clear is that the most effective prevention messages are those that have clear, well-defined aims, are relevant to the audience, and are sustained and consistent. Prevention strategy can encompass a wide range of tools to help deliver this. In the UK the Drug Prevention Advisory Service (DPAS) was established as an interface between the government and offices that can deliver prevention. It ensures that all prevention material and information conform to the four strands of the UK's anti-drugs strategy, which includes education and prevention.

EFFECTIVE HEROIN PREVENTION

- Should have a well-defined purpose
- Needs to be relevant to the audience
- Should include the most accurate and the most up-to-the-minute information
- The messages need to be credible and delivered through credible sources such as youth services
- They should also challenge stereotypes
- Delivery needs to be through a well-thought-out plan, repeated often, but in a variety of imaginative ways
- Should be built on existing values and should reinforce existing anti-drug beliefs

At one end of the scale, prevention may also include harm reduction approaches, which are particularly appropriate for needle-using heroin users. These might include prevention strategies to reduce the likelihood of succumbing to a drug overdose by offering resuscitation and awareness training to addicts or providing more access to methadone treatment, the established medication of choice for treating heroin addiction.

Prevention could also involve reducing the risk of HIV or hepatitis and will include the provision of information on sterilizing injecting equipment and making clean syringes more widely available.

An August 2001 consultation document addressing drug prevention approaches suggested that the routes leading users towards heroin and addiction are so complex that several prevention strategies need to be developed.

Written by David Best and John Witton of the UK's National Addiction Centre, *Guidelines For Drug Prevention* suggested that prevention can fall into two distinct groups: universal and targeted programmes. The former approach aims to reach the general population or a wide cross-section of society, and will include awareness campaigns and anti-drug education programmes, possibly at school.

The elements of school prevention are essentially the same throughout the world and will include a mix of drug education classes, school visits by drug experts, social workers, former users or law enforcement. Results from the USA show that because two-thirds of all initiation to drug use in 1998 took place mostly during the school years – 12 to 17 years old – substance prevention programmes in the classroom are vital.

> 'Heroin is actually a benign drug. It doesn't attack the organs of the body. The problems come about from sharing syringes and we need to focus the message that most of the dangers are associated with the lifestyle.' Gary Sutton, heroin project adviser, Release

However, Shapiro admits that the quality of drug information in schools varies enormously 'from the local police officer coming in for a chat, to the school putting on a play about the issues'. The level that messages should be pitched at is also hard to gauge because, within a class of 30 children, some will know nothing about drugs, some may be using drugs and others will think they know everything, but probably don't. Drug information in schools also flies in the face of how kids are normally taught. They are presented with drug information and asked to make up their own minds, but throughout the rest of the school curriculum they are told exactly what to do and how to behave.

There is a school of thought that prevention strategy in classrooms should accept drug experimentation as a given and concentrate mostly on how children can protect themselves and be safe if they use drugs. Shapiro accepts this is an option, but says the moral climate and opposition from some politicians, parents and teachers is unlikely to see this accepted in the short term. 'I'm not sure teachers are going to be comfortable teaching kids how to inject,' he says.

Presenting a credible message to media-savvy children is also a problem faced by teachers. Gary Sutton, heroin project adviser at Release, doesn't believe enough is made of former drug addicts going into schools. Sutton argues that at the very least they can provide a credible message because they have been through heroin addiction, but believes the problem for schools asking outsiders to come in is that this may be seen as a tacit admission that the school has a drug problem. Sutton adds, 'Unless there is a borough-wide policy, then certain headmasters will be nervous because the implication of having a drug addict visit is that heroin or other drugs are used at that school and that has obvious implications for parents and school governors.'

Media campaigns also fall within the universal programme, and their role in drug prevention is to inform people about the services on offer, influence opinion formers and also create a climate where drugs are discussed. However, there has been extensive debate about the use and effectiveness of campaigns, especially in the UK.

> 'Shock tactics like the "Heroin Screws You Up" campaign don't work. An image like that is so far removed from people's lives. Their networks are with friends. Their parents could have a drug problem, they could have mental problems. A photo of someone with a needle in their arm isn't part of their experience. We aim to build people's self-esteem because telling people not to take drugs doesn't work. You need to identify the people at risk and build up their self-esteem.' Claire Moore, fundraising manager, Action on Addiction

The UK's first national drug campaign came about in the mid-1980s. It featured heroin. Prior to that, heroin wasn't seen as being near the top of the political agenda because until the late 1970s there was a fairly stable and older injecting community. However, in the early 1980s there was an influx of smokable heroin.

The response of the Conservative government, which came in 1984, was to create a ministerial group chaired by the then Home Office minister David Mellor to create a strategy to stamp out heroin. This sparked one of the most high-profile and controversial episodes of Prime Minister Margaret Thatcher's political reign. The Department of Health and Social Security (DHSS) and the Central Office of Information (COI) approached Yellowhammer, an ambitious advertising agency based in London's West End to produce a high-profile poster and press campaign aimed specifically at heroin users.

The images the agency produced were designed to shock. Under the white-on-black strapline 'Heroin Screws You Up', one showed a teenager in jeans and sweat-soaked shirt hunched up, his mouth pressed against his filthy hands and fingernails. 'Your Mind Isn't The Only Thing Heroin Damages' it warned, alongside seven well-documented by-products of heavy heroin use, including skin infections, wasted muscles and liver complaints. The copy was equally hard-hitting: 'You'll begin to take heroin not to get high any more, but just to feel normal. And, as you lose control of your body's health, you could lose control of your mind too. Until one day you'll wake up knowing that, instead of you controlling heroin, it now controls you.'

The same image accompanied by the same side effects – mental problems, skin infections, blood diseases, constipation – associated with long-term heroin addicts was given another eye-catching strapline – 'How Low Can You Get On Heroin' – followed by the no-holds-barred copy 'Take heroin and before long you'll start looking ill, losing weight and feeling like death. So, if you're offered heroin, you know what to say.'

Another teenager, with dark rings under his eyes, spotty skin and a lank fringe, peered from another bleak ad. This strapline read 'Skin Care By Heroin'. Other ads used another withdrawn-looking male model and the line 'All He Wanted Was A Few Laughs'; one of the few ads using a female model had the copyline 'How You React Could Decide Whether She Rejects Drugs Or You'. Later the campaign was used in women's magazines to target mothers, whom the agency had identified in its research as the most important figure in the family for dealing with drug-related problems.

The campaign appeared at the same time as the street price of heroin had fallen, making heroin cheaper than some soft drugs and bringing in a new market of kids willing to smoke the drug. Few campaigns have attracted as much public attention as the £2 million ($2.9 million) Yellowhammer campaign, which appealed to adolescent vanity. At the time Sammy Harari, the board account director at the ad agency responsible for the campaign, said, 'All this campaign is trying to do is to begin to shift people's attitudes.'

THE 'HEROIN SCREWS YOU UP' ADVERTISING CAMPAIGN
ARGUMENTS FOR
- Used as effective part of overall drug strategy, advertising is a persuasive instrument
- Helps increase information provision
- Is high profile

ARGUMENTS AGAINST
- Advertising has no effect on behaviour
- Unable to reach target groups
- Seems to be 'marketing' drugs
- Simplistic
- Glamorizes heroin and encourages anti-establishment teenagers to try it

The advantages of advertising and other universal programmes are that they don't label or stigmatize individuals and they may provide the groundwork for targeted programmes. However, it is often difficult to measure the effectiveness of broad prevention strategies and there doesn't appear to be any robust scientific evidence to show they work or have any lasting impact.

Drug experts suggested that the 'Heroin Screws You Up' campaign, for example, would only put off people who wouldn't try the drug anyway and wouldn't necessarily impact that much on those people who are already using. In other words, it may have the greatest effect on those at lowest risk.

The advertising also drew criticism from drug charity workers and other experts, who thought that it may actually be counter-productive because young people would be drawn to the grunge images. They argued that the ad campaign was too simplistic because the posters gave the impression that people end up a mess if they take heroin, whereas the reality is that heroin is just one part of a combination of factors including drink and social circumstance. Therefore, they argued that it is better to spend the money on education in schools and throughout communities because then subtleties can be raised and understood.

The campaign also caused some problems for health workers. It scared many parents who thought that the onset of spots on their teenager's face meant they were on heroin. Heroin was being blamed for every problem in a family, even if no member of that family was actually taking it.

Significantly, this kind of campaign may also have the opposite effect to that it sets out to achieve. Teenagers are predominantly anti-establishment, and there was anecdotal evidence that many found the emaciated models accompanied by the tough copylines attractive because they were seen as a product of the establishment machine. The poster featuring the adolescent boy was a favourite of students, who hung it in their bedrooms next to posters of Nick Cave and David Bowie.

TABLE 4.3: REASONS GIVEN FOR NOT USING HEROIN

Fear of physical harm	35%
Fear of addiction	32%
Fear of the effects	27%
Lack of interest in the effects	22%
Having seen the effect on others	16%
Cost	9%
Unfamiliarity with the drug	4%

Sources: Fountain, J *et al* (1999): 'Why Say No? Reasons Given By Young People For Not Using Drugs'; Boys *et al* (2000) 'Drugs Decisions: A Qualitative Study Of Young People'

More recently, a UK media campaign featuring a young victim of heroin put the drug on the political agenda again. It showed the corpse of Rachel Whitear, which had lain slumped in a bedsit for several days after she had suffered an overdose. The image was undeniably powerful and garnered extensive national coverage on television and in newspapers.

However, there were many dissenting voices. Opponents of this and similar shock tactics argue it is scattergun scaremongering, rarely targeting users or potential users or communicating hard information about minimizing the effects of the drug or treatment. Also, because several similar campaigns have targeted heroin, some drug experts believe they give the impression that other Class A drugs, such as cocaine, are less harmful.

Thinking about prevention tactics in the early 2000s began to swing towards more targeted programmes, which aim to reduce the influence of the risk factors that lead people to heroin and build on creating coping strategies or other skills. Shapiro says, 'This one-size-fits-all campaign improves the profile of things, but it doesn't have that much impact. People don't change until they see they are at immediate risk.'

Best and Witton also believe targeted prevention programmes will single out the individuals who are most susceptible to drug misuse and suggest they have the potential to catch misuse early and are an efficient tool for directing resources to tackle the problem.

However, the biggest headaches arising from these methods are the difficulties associated with accurate targeting, cost and increasing the risk of stigmatization. They also ignore the wider social context that has led a user to drugs.

Targeted approaches can again encompass a wide variety of projects and drug support groups. For some heroin users they may involve the family or peer group. For example, if it is discovered that the addict is taking heroin because of pressure from friends, then a project could be developed to remove or reduce peer-group influence.

Sutton adds that both universal and targeted approaches always need to be used in conjunction with one another. 'We need to offer alternatives,' he says. 'Not just for preventing heroin use because people drift into drug use because they don't have anything else in their lives. The alternative is to provide a different path, but of course it is very expensive to provide youth clubs and activities, which give young people a direction.'

Evidence from the US does seem to suggest that mass-media prevention campaigns are having some success. Following the UNDCP's 1997 $200 million (£138 million) National Youth Anti-Drug Campaign, which used more targeted approaches, drug use in US schools fell away from an alarming upward swing. The Monitoring the Future studies group, which collects data on US school students, found that drug use among 14-year-old eighth-grade students fell in the USA between 1996 and 1999 by 12 per cent.

FIRST PERSON
MARK McLEAN – NATIONAL DRUGS HELPLINE MANAGER
'We receive between 250,000 and 300,000 calls each year. It's a free and confidential service and then the National Drugs Helpline (NDH) refers one in five callers to drug agencies.

'We take more calls about heroin than any other drug. I'd say a quarter of our calls relate to heroin. After the death of Rachel Whitear we had lots of calls from parents. Parents respond more to stories like this than young people. Our remit is not to lobby the government or influence policy. We're like an older brother or sister to the young people who contact us. We're not judgmental, we don't tell them to get off drugs. We point out the legal risks and health risks associated with heroin or any other drug. People are going to take heroin anyway and our job is to advise them how to inject, to use clean needles, to avoid contaminated heroin, and also how to minimize harm.

'Campaigns like the "Heroin Screws You Up" advertising have the government stamped all over them, and for that reason are less credible among young people. The face of the person on the poster doesn't match the face of their mate who uses heroin so they aren't likely to trust the campaign.

'"Heroin Screws You Up" had an impact because people still remember it, but whether it has an impact on behaviour is debatable. The key for the campaigns we're involved in is to promote the services we offer and for that reason campaigns have to be credible and constructive, and direct people to information and support.'

HEROIN TREATMENT
When governments construct their drug budgets there is always a trade-off between how much they will spend on treatment and the resources put into tackling drug crime. For most of the last century, law and order has been the priority and so in the UK in 1998 only 13 per cent of the £1.4 billion ($2 billion) spent on drug-related activity went towards treatment.

However, the amount spent on treatment in most countries is generally increasing, boosted by the growing conviction that there is a better chance of winning the war on drugs if addicts are given treatment instead of punishment. Results from the USA also back up those who favour treatment over legislation. The US SAMHSA National Treatment Improvement Study 1996, which investigated the effectiveness of publicly funded drug treatment, discovered that there was a 47 per cent decline in heroin use one year after treatment ended.

> 'The nature of drug dependency is it creeps up on you. People use drugs because they enjoy them, even heroin, and for a while they will be in control of it rather than it being in control of them. But gradually it will come to control them. It typically takes a number of years before the penny drops and they begin to see the drug as a net negative rather than net benefit.' - Paul Hayes, chief executive of the UK National Treatment Agency

Another US report, the *Drug Abuse Treatment Outcome Studies* conducted on behalf of the USA National Institute on Drug Abuse (NIDA) in the 1990s, also confirmed that treatment could significantly curb hardcore heroin use. One year after the end of treatment the study found that consumption levels of heroin had fallen by about two-thirds.

In May 2002, the UK's Association of Chief Police Officers (ACPO) issued new proposals suggesting that, in some circumstances, treatment for heroin addiction should be considered as an alternative to prosecution. The ACPO report said it looked forward to the time when those who appear in court for misuse of Class A drugs, such as heroin, have immediate access to treatment.

Spending on drugs misuse in the UK was £700 million ($1 billion) in 2000/01 and expected to rise to £1 billion ($1.5 billion) in 2003/04. Of this, £234 million ($340 million) was spent on treatment in 2001/02, rising to over £400 million ($580 million) in 2003/04. Of this, the UK's National Treatment Agency (NTA), which is a joint initiative between the Home Office and the National Health Service to improve the quality and quantity of drug treatment, had a £234 million ($340 million) annual budget. By 2003 the NTA was expecting to have £400 million ($580 million) to spend on treatment, with funds significantly increasing until 2008.

In addition to this, £32 million ($46.5 million) was spent on young people and prevention work in 2001/02, due to rise to £71 million ($103 million) in 2003/04.

Any intervention – from providing better housing to creating jobs – that makes someone less likely to use heroin can be defined as treatment. However, health organizations normally focus on a much narrower definition of treatment, which is essentially providing healthcare and counselling.

There are many different care pathways for kicking a heroin habit. Some are more successful than others, and they can be delivered in a variety of ways. Many are also used in tandem. The NTA boils the main methods down to five:

1   counselling
2   day centre
3   detoxification
4   prescribing
5   residential

These can be delivered by and through a bewildering array of different services and agencies, which may vary slightly throughout the world depending on factors that include the policies of national and local government and the health authorities.

TABLE 4.4: HEROIN TREATMENT

	NUMBER OF ADMISSIONS	YEAR
Italy	121,000	1997
France (opiates including heroin)	94,400	1997
Switzerland	19,000	1998
The Netherlands	19,000	1999
USA	216,900	1998

However, the first port of call for an addict wanting to quit a habit will probably be a call to their countries' national drugs helpline, such as

Narcotics Anonymous. This is likely to give confidential free advice 24 hours a day, and can put the heroin user in touch with other local agencies or groups. When someone is arrested they can also be routed towards drug agencies if they need treatment.

The family doctor or local hospital will also offer help to addicts trying to kick smack. In the UK, doctors make more referrals to specialist drug services than any other point of contact. The doctor can usually provide advice, sometimes prescribe substitute drugs, sometimes – although very rarely – prescribe heroin, often in tandem with a wide network of other specialist agencies and services.

> Studies show that every $1 (70p) spent on treatment produces saving on crime costs of around $2 (£1.40).

There will also be a huge variety of different drug agencies, volunteer services, street agencies and community drug teams (which are multidisciplinary teams including counsellors, psychiatrists, social workers and advice services via the phone, drop-in centres or home visits). These confidential services will probably not simply confine themselves to the user, but will also involve the user's partner and friends.

Some may also have their own doctors, who may be able to prescribe drugs for detox or maintenance programmes and, if necessary, will steer the heroin user to other more appropriate services.

The quality of counselling and the qualifications of those providing it can vary, but these services are essentially designed to determine how serious users are about ridding themselves of their habits and to point them in the right direction to facilitate this.

> 'Our researchers have shown that for every £1 [$1.45] spent on drug treatment, we save £3 [$4.35] in terms of crime.'
> Lesley King-Lewis, chief executive of Action on Addiction, which claims that one in three adults in the UK suffers from some form of addiction

The street agencies and drug teams will also probably provide aftercare treatment, possibly combined with home visits or group therapy.

Syringe- and needle-exchange facilities are also available in many countries, including the UK, which pioneered their introduction in the 1980s. They provide clean works to heroin and other drug injectors, and are designed to stop the spread of HIV and other blood-borne viruses such as hepatitis C. Many are sited near drug advice projects or hospitals, and some have their own confidential advice services and counsellors. Gary Sutton, heroin project adviser at Release, says he believes there is no proof that needle exchanges will increase the number of addicts on the streets, and that they have been 'absolutely central' in halting the spread of HIV in the UK. Outreach services will also attempt to bring the service to the user and may include a needle exchange and counselling service going into a heroin user's home

Hospital-based drug dependency units services are normally available for people who are heavy, long-term heroin users. Drug dependency units are usually based within a hospital and provide another level of services on top of counselling, advice and information. These may include psychiatric treatment, advice on better syringe practice, needle exchange and home visits. Some may also offer a prescribing service and a detox service. Most can prescribe substitute drugs, such as methadone, in reducing script or maintenance programmes to stabilize the addict.

> A total of 837,000 people were admitted into US treatment in 1998, the majority for cocaine abuse. The 216,000 admissions to treatment for heroin abuse in the USA in 1998 were equivalent to 22 per cent of the estimated 980,000 hardcore heroin users.

Treatments can vary in different countries or even in different regions of a country, but will usually require a referral from a doctor or social worker. There is normally a waiting list.

Residential rehabilitation centres are also sometimes available for longer-term heroin users. Some offer detoxification on the premises, but most are only open to those who have already been through detox and are drug free. The addict will live in these rehabs for several months or more in a bid to kick their habit, although length of stay is often determined by costs, which are often very high. There are several types of programme available, but for heroin use the main ones tend to be based on the 'Minnesota model', which sees addicts work through a stepped programme, or a therapeutic approach, which includes intense therapy sessions.

FIRST PERSON

EDDIE COWLEY, DRUGS ARREST REFERRAL WORKER

'A lot of young drug users are in a terrible mess and it's very disheartening. Sometimes I want to pack it all in and become a dustman, but I carry on because I'd like to think I can do some good. It's a result when anyone gets off heroin but it's also a result to see someone clean and healthy even if they're still using.

'When someone is arrested they are asked if they want to see a drugs worker, irrespective of the offence. This is a Home Office initiative aimed at tackling criminal behaviour that is motivated by drugs. If the person in the cells says "yes", I go in to the police station to see them and assess the problem, and refer them to drug agencies if they need further treatment. Drug users' problems vary – they could be jobless, homeless or maybe they have family problems. The referral process can take six to eight months, which is far too long.

'There are various options open to us within the criminal justice system. The Drug Treatment & Testing Orders (DTTOs) are mostly targeted at heroin users. People committing crimes to feed their habit are put on a DTTO and assigned a worker. They are put on a methadone programme and tested regularly. The programme is designed to keep them out of prison. The problem is that you have to be arrested before you can get on to this type of programme. Unless you've broken the law you can't get help.

'Methadone is prescribed in different ways. First, there is maintenance prescribing script in which users sign a contract and go on to a methadone programme. These tend to be long-term users. The problem with methadone is that it's very addictive. Drug users generally don't like it because it zonks them out completely. But at the moment methadone is all that's available for drug agencies.

'Second, there is the reduction prescribing script for people who want to come off heroin and methadone. The methadone dose is gradually reduced. Finally, there is the maintenance prescribing script with a view to detoxing. This is a residential detoxing programme and tends to be aimed at older people in their late twenties and thirties. Young people normally haven't finished their drugs career and aren't receptive to this particular remedy.

Methadone, an opiate analgesic that can be substituted for opioid drugs such as heroin, mimicking their effects and so helping to combat withdrawal symptoms. When a drug addict is treated with methadone, the dose must gradually be reduced with time, as methadone itself is highly addictive.

Ophthalmoscope's view of the retina of a patient's eye that has been damaged by chronic heroin use. The macula (CENTRE), where most of the eye's light-sensitive cells are found, is seen as a dark-coloured spot. A small light patch to the right of the macula is a clump of light-sensitive cells that have been damaged by the heroin abuse. This kind of degeneration is called *retinal maculopathy* and can lead to damaged vision, even blindness.

A scene from Otto Preminger's 1955 film *The Man With The Golden Arm*, which exploded the taboo surrounding narcotics abuse, with Frank Sinatra portraying heroin addict and jazz drummer Frankie Machine. The film was in violation of the PCA, which refused to grant it a certificate, and so Preminger released the film himself. Its success helped convince the PCA to amend its code a year later to allow treatments of drug addiction to be shown. Although the audience never gets to see the needle in Sinatra's arm, he is seen preparing to tie off a tourniquet and the camera lingers on his face as the rush hits.

William Burroughs, junky turned novelist, who died in 1984 at the age of 83. A contemporary of Jack Kerouac and Allen Ginsberg, Burroughs was an influential member of the 'beat generation'. His work *Naked Lunch* caused such a scandal when it was written, in 1959, that it wasn't published until three years later.

Actress James King, who first appeared in a Davide Sorrenti photograph typifying heroin chic.

Alice In Chains vocalist Layne Staley, one of rock's many heroin casualties

'I think the government genuinely does want to do something, but the money gets distributed in the wrong way. Services for people with drug problems are incredibly limited. The government concentrates too much on punitive measures and not rehabilitation and it isn't addressing the social causes of why people take heroin. Votes have a lot to do with it. The government wants to tackle crime figures rather than dealing with the underlying problems of heroin abuse.'

TYPES OF TREATMENT

Once a heroin addict has approached one of the main agencies or services for help, it will point him towards one or more of a whole range of treatment types and delivery models that are available. Again, different care and treatment types exist around the world, but the NTA's experience in the UK is typical.

In 2002, there were 120,000 people in drug treatment in the UK, approximately 100,000 of whom were heroin and opiate users. The NTA had set a target to have 200,000 entering treatment in 2008. However, treatments are really only successful when the heroin user wants to give up the drug and is not simply succumbing to pressure from a husband, wife or other family member or has been forced to reassess use because they are facing a prison term. There is no simple cure for heroin addiction and the user must decide for themselves that the drug is taking over – often ruining – their lives and they need help.

Treatment is also more effective if abuse is identified early. But in the early months and years of abuse many heroin users may not have been sucked into the debilitating side effects of the drug. It is only when their health suffers, they lose their jobs, homes and family or contract HIV that they turn to help. Accessing people earlier also aids the efficacy of the resources ranged against drug addiction because younger people are more able to detox, whereas heroin users in their later twenties or early thirties often need methadone maintenance to first stabilize them, and that clogs the system.

Some evidence suggests that the method of administration may dictate how long a user waits before they ask for help. According to the US

Substance Abuse and Mental Health Services Administration (SAMHSA) *Treatment Episode Data Set 2001* those who inhaled heroin in 1998 sought treatment sooner than heroin injectors. On average, those snorting or smoking heroin sought treatment after six years. Injectors waited until they had been using a needle for about 11 years before seeking treatment.

More success is likely to result when agencies and services are combined or cooperate to offer the addict a multidisciplined treatment. Thus, if a heroin user is trying to kick the drug with methadone at a residential clinic, then specialist drug workers should offer support when he returns home. Perhaps a support network of other past users will also operate in his area and he should be encouraged to attend.

In 2002 the NTA was seeking to introduce a Models of Care system, which would provide an integrated system for the heroin addict and highlight clearer care pathways. Someone would be responsible for determining the optimal route of treatment for an individual and also appointed to manage the whole 'journey' of an addict, through counselling, to detox or prescription.

According to Best and Witton, evidence also shows that the greatest gains are likely to result from longer stays in treatment. Other factors that could impact on the success of heroin treatment are whether the patient is allowed to take methadone home and the type of regime offered. They suggest that the treatment is likely to be more successful the more control the addict has.

METHADONE REDUCTION AND MAINTENANCE PROGRAMMES

Methadone, a synthetic opiate usually taken orally, is used in heroin replacement treatments. It induces less euphoria and blocks opioid receptors in the brain, avoiding withdrawal. It stabilizes the patient and reduces risks to their health in preparation for counselling, group work and reintegration into the community.

The effectiveness of treatment is largely dependent on the quality of the treatment and also the commitment of the addict taking part. Properly prescribed methadone is not intoxicating or sedating, and its effects do not interfere with ordinary activities such as driving a car.

The medication can suppress narcotic withdrawal for 24 to 36 hours, and patients are able to perceive pain and have emotional reactions. Most important, methadone relieves the craving associated with heroin addiction; craving is a major reason for relapse. Methadone's effects last for about 24 hours – four to six times as long as those of heroin – so people in treatment need take it only once a day.

Methadone is used as a replacement for heroin in treatments aimed at either maintenance or gradual withdrawal. The reduction method is not particularly new and was suggested to help wean opium addicts off the drug in Thailand in the early 1800s. But the modern treatment model was devised by the American physicians Professor Vincent Dole and Marie Nyswander in 1964. Methadone reduction treatment usually takes place in community settings and is designed to help the user withdraw or detoxify completely from opioid use. The aim is to gradually reduce the quantity prescribed until the user experiences no withdrawal symptoms and is drug free. The degree of reduction and length of time used to achieve abstinence can vary from a few weeks to many months, and motivation is the key to the success of these programmes.

Methadone maintenance treatment is a form of respite care, maintaining users by prescribing the drug to stabilize them. Methadone is medically safe even when used continuously for ten years or more. The theory behind the treatment is that methadone maintenance reduces some of the criminality associated with heroin and, because it is usually delivered in community settings, removes the risk of infection and enables those on the programme to live a normal life. In 2000 about 150,000 people were on methadone maintenance programmes in the USA, however methadone does not automatically convert a heroin addict into a law-abiding citizen and must be backed up with aftercare, which can plug the abuser into a new, more fulfilling, way of life.

Those opposed to methadone replacement argue that there is little evidence to suggest that criminal behaviour has been reduced or that those on programmes have been successful at finding work. Also, because it replaces one drug with another, it is not perceived as being a cure and, often, some methadone will find its way on to the black market.

Many heroin users approach methadone treatments, which have no aftercare or back-up, as simply another drug supply – a pharmacological stop-gap – and when they can't find a ready supply of smack they will take the next available drug.

The US Substance Abuse and Mental Health Services Administration (SAMHSA) *Treatment Episode Data Set 2001* also found that heroin inhalers

The estimated number of global opiate abuses is 13.5 million.

were less likely than heroin injectors to receive methadone treatment. The use of methadone as part of treatment generally declined for both heroin injectors and inhalers from 1993 to 1998. The number of injectors on methadone fell from just over 60 per cent to less than 50 per cent and, for inhalers, from less than 50 per cent to 25 per cent in 1997.

Methadone remains the most widely used narcotic in treatment, but in recent years other synthetic drugs have been tested and in some countries, such as Australia and France, have been introduced into narcotic detoxification and maintenance therapy programmes as an alternative to methadone.

Buprenorphine was previously available for treating severe pain and its use in narcotic addiction is now spreading rapidly. A man-made narcotic, it is the least addictive powerful narcotic, and both an agonist and a blocker of the opioid nerve receptors. This means that it provides a moderate narcotic effect and blocks the craving for and effects of other narcotics.

Buprenorphine also produces a lower level of physical dependence, which means that patients who discontinue medication generally have fewer withdrawal symptoms than those who stop taking methadone. Because of these advantages, buprenorphine is also more appropriate for use in a wider variety of treatment settings.

Naloxone and naltrexone are medications that also block the effects of morphine, heroin and other opiates. As antagonists, they are especially useful as antidotes. Naltrexone has long-lasting effects, ranging from one to three days, depending on the dose. It blocks the pleasurable effects of heroin and is useful in treating some highly motivated individuals.

Naltrexone has also been found to be successful in preventing relapse by former opiate addicts released from prison.

OPIATE DETOXIFICATION

The primary objective of detoxification is to relieve withdrawal symptoms while patients adjust to a drug-free state. Not in itself a treatment for addiction, detoxification is a useful step only when it leads into long-term treatment that is either drug free (residential or out-patient) or uses medications as part of the treatment. The best-documented drug-free treatments are the therapeutic community residential programmes lasting at least three to six months.

However, it has also been known for some users to detox at home where the addict simply stops taking dope and goes through four or five days of painful withdrawal symptoms. The heroin user should cut down their dose to the minimum just prior to detox and make themselves comfortable, usually in bed. They should eat well and take cool showers and plenty of liquids. A family member or friend should also be enlisted to help out. However, even in a special detox unit there may be some suffering and often a high failure rate. There is also a high risk of OD if the detox fails and the heroin user returns to the streets for another score.

HEROIN PRESCRIBING

Heroin prescribing is available in several countries with more liberal attitudes towards heroin treatment, including the UK, The Netherlands, Australia, Switzerland, and Spain. Before May 2002 there were only about 30 doctors in the UK who were still prescribing heroin to around 300 heroin users under licence (the government had stopped wholesale prescribing in 1968).

However, in early 2002 the NTA announced that it would examine the efficacy of reintroducing a wider system of prescribing heroin. Chief executive Paul Hayes said there were around 5 to 10 per cent of heroin users who didn't respond well to methadone and would probably do better on prescribed diamorphine. However, he conceded that the 'willingness of doctors is not great' and there were a number of issues that the treatment agency needed to address. 'There are cost implications because it is much more expensive. People have to use three times a day for the rest of their lives. And we've got to make sure it doesn't leak on to the market like it did in the 1960s and make sure we are not entrenching people in injecting behaviour. It is not an easy solution, but I'm pretty sure it's got a role to play,' he said.

Support for heroin prescribing also came from the UK police. In 2001 the Association of Chief Police Officers (ACPO) called for the mass prescription of heroin to addicts through specialist units in police stations, GPs' surgeries and hospitals. This would ensure that addicts had clean needles and health advice, and would keep contaminated needles off the street. ACPO president Sir David Phillips said at the time, 'The system has failed. We have an out-of-control drugs industry and it is time to try a new approach.' However, an ACPO spokesman said, 'It's not about legalizing heroin, but just the possibility of having heroin monitored and regulated from police stations.'

The Royal College of General Practitioners, however, voiced concerns about heroin prescribing in the UK in 2002. The college claimed it had a low therapeutic index and for a user who has lost their tolerance may be fatal. It also suggested it was too expensive, claiming that one year of methadone treatment cost £2,000 ($3,000) compared to around £10,000–15,000 ($14,500–22,000) for heroin.

Despite this, the UK drugs inquiry by the House of Commons Home Affairs Select Committee, chaired by Chris Mullin, recommended in May 2002 that a nationwide network of 'safe injecting areas' should be set up, with medical heroin prescribed by the National Health Service. Models of how heroin prescribing could be achieved were also being examined by the NTA.

Supervised consumption needs to be open at times that users can access it – usually late at night – and should also be secure so that drugs cannot be supplied to the illegal market. Often called 'shooting galleries', clinics where addicts can go for a health check, with provision for injecting and resuscitation equipment, have been piloted and used in Australia, Switzerland, Germany, and other parts of Europe.

Switzerland's large-scale, long-term heroin maintenance experiment, in which a number of addicts were given regular doses of heroin under controlled conditions, has resulted in some dramatic results. Ueli Minder of the Swiss Federal Office of Public Health said it has been accompanied by a fall in homelessness, a major reduction in illicit heroin and cocaine use, an improvement in the employment rate (in the treatment group) from 14 per cent to 32 per cent, and an eventual significant switch to other, more conventional treatments such as methadone maintenance and abstinence therapy.

Encouraged by five-year trials, the Dutch government also asked its parliament in March 2002 to endorse proposals to hand out heroin in combination with methadone to addicts who were 'beyond help'.

Sutton is in favour of shooting galleries because he says they reduce the visibility of addicts hanging around street corners and also the prevalence of discarded syringes. However, there are associated problems, he says. 'There are always people who don't want these things in their backyard. Also, how many addicts will go to a shooting gallery three times each day? But the alternative to shooting galleries is people's homes and you have to weigh the social consequences. What is the most damaging?'

Hayes said it would be unlikely that heroin prescribing would become the main form of medical treatment for heroin addiction. 'Methadone is likely to remain the most appropriate form of treatment for the majority of cases. There are, however, users who are not accessing treatment either because they have not responded well to the use of methadone, or because they refuse this form of treatment.' He proposed that heroin prescribing could be used as a 'gateway treatment' to encourage users to enter other forms of treatment.

He also conceded that politics and the media play an important part in these treatments being made available. 'If there was a political move that this wasn't on, then it would be more difficult to achieve it,' he said. 'Certainly from our point of view we are being told to follow evidence. And if the evidence shows X works, then we want more X, whatever it is.'

BEHAVIOURAL THERAPIES

Although behavioural and pharmacologic treatments can be extremely useful when employed alone, integrating both types of treatment will ultimately produce the most effective results. There are many effective behavioural treatments available for heroin addiction, which can include residential and out-patient approaches. An important task is to match the best treatment approach to the particular needs of the patient.

Several new behavioural therapies, such as contingency management therapy and cognitive-behavioural interventions, have been developed with some success for heroin addiction. Contingency management therapy uses a voucher-based system, where patients earn 'points' based on negative drug tests, which they can exchange for items that encourage healthy living.

The cognitive behavioural interventions are designed to help modify the patient's thinking, expectancies and behaviour and to increase skills in coping with various stress factors they encounter in the real world.

227,000 regular UK heroin users consume an estimated 30 tonnes of the drug annually, with a street value of £2.3 billion ($3.3 billion).

HEROIN MONEY

Like all commodities, heroin's market value goes up or down depending on a series of factors, such as the supply of opium, the size of the user market and its demand, cost of smuggling and the scale of the profits taken by the crime organizations handling the drug. The National Criminal Intelligence Service estimated in 2002 that the mark-up on a kilo [2¼lb] of heroin was between £130,000 and £250,000 [$190,000 and $360,000], depending on the size of the drug-trafficking organization.

US research by the Office of National Drug Control Policy shows that heroin is getting cheaper. The 2001 study, *The Price Of Illicit Drugs*, shows that in the early 1980s, users were spending up to $5 (£3.45) per milligram, but by the 2000s they were spending closer to $0.40 (28p) per milligram.

TABLE 5.1: ESTIMATED HEROIN PRICE PER PURE GRAM AT FOUR PURCHASE LEVELS

	1981	2000
Wholesale distributor (more than 10 grams)	$915.95	$119.16
Mid-level distributor (1 to 10 grams)	$1,167.53	$282.83
Large user (between 0.1 and 1 gram)	$2,100.92	$411.02
Small user (less than 0.1 grams)	£3,339.52	$2,114.49

Note: $1 = 70p (approx)/10g = ⅓oz
Source: US Office of National Drug Control Policy

Heroin prices have fluctuated enormously since the beginning of the 1990s, partly due to law enforcement and the influence of governments in the main opium poppy regions. But one of the main catalysts has been the wars fought in Afghanistan. In the early 1990s when the civil war in the country was at its height and opium production went unfettered, 1kg (2¼lb) of raw opium fetched around $40 (£28) on the open market.

A gram of heroin in London costs about £50 ($72), $40–60 (£28–41) in New York, AUS$100–120 (£38–46/$55–67) in Sydney and around 98 euros (£63/$91) in Paris.

With the Taliban gaining power, the price of Afghan opium – and therefore heroin – remained relatively stable. However, the regime's ban on poppy growing in 2000 sent the price of opium up to about $800 (£552) per kilo (2¼lb). The price crashed back to around $500 (£345) and stabilized in 2002 when the USA led attacks against the Taliban and Osama bin Laden in Afghanistan because opium farmers began planting again.

However, despite the massive fall in the production of opium it had little effect on prices in the UK and other European countries that are serviced by Afghan heroin. This was because producers had stockpiled supplies following a bumper crop in 1999 to keep supplies – and prices – level, although Luxembourg, Portugal, Sweden, and the UK reported a slight decrease in 1999.

By 2002 there were signs that this was changing, with reports from users that the quality of heroin was dropping and the cost expected to increase. According to Addiction, the UK's biggest treatment charity, the cost of a gram in London, traditionally the most expensive market, was £60 ($87) in 2002. In other major UK cities, such as Birmingham, a gram could be bought for around £40 to £50 ($58 to $72).

Finding out how much the heroin market is actually worth in different countries is a difficult proposition, but in 2001 the UK Home Office attempted to put a value on it. The *Sizing The UK Market For Illicit Drugs* report (see Table 5.2), by the National Economic Research Associates for the Home Office, estimated that there were 270,000 regular heroin users in England and Wales, some 25,329 occasional users and several thousand in the prison population.

Assuming a regular heroin user, who on average used the drug on 24.6 days in the last 30, and spends about £28.80 ($42) per day on heroin, equates to an annual drugs bill of £8,516 ($12,340). However, because heroin users are often poly-drug users (the report cited that 53 per cent of regular heroin users also used crack cocaine and 24 per cent were regular cocaine users; also, almost 20 per cent of regular heroin users were regular users of both crack and cocaine; the

On the streets, heroin prices varied between £18 and £208 ($26 and $300) per gram in 1999 across the EU with the highest prices expected to be paid in Finland and Sweden.

vast majority of regular crack users – 83 per cent – were also regular heroin users) the report suggested they would spend a total of around £16,500 ($24,000) per year. It was, therefore, able to estimate that the total market for illicit drugs was £6.6 billion ($9.6 billion), with the heroin market easily the biggest part of that at £2.31 billion ($3.35 billion).

TABLE 5.2: ILLICIT DRUG MARKET

TYPE OF HEROIN USER	NUMBER	SPEND
Regular	270,097	£2,299.9m
Occasional	25,329	£1.4m
Prison	3,331	£11.7m

TYPE OF DRUG	TOTAL VALUE OF MARKET
Heroin	£2,313m
Amphetamines	£257.7m
Cannabis	£1,577.9m
Cocaine	£352.8m
Crack	£1,817.4m
Ecstasy	£294.6m
Total value of illicit drug market	£6,613.5m

Note: £1 = $1.45 (approx)
Source: *Sizing The UK Market For Illicit Drugs*

FIRST PERSON

STEVE C, HEROIN DEALER

'Most of my weeks are pretty much the same, but I guess this one started when I got fucked up last night. I played pool with a few mates and did a bit of business. I always do a bit of business. Always. I'm on all the fucking time, can't miss a trick. Besides I know everyone down the pool hall. They know I deal, but I don't do it on the premises. Frank, he usually runs the place weekends. He probably wouldn't mind, but I always do it outside. That's where I make the trade.

'I was just playing pool, drinking a bit. Frank shuts up around three in the morning, so I guess we left around then. I don't just deal heroin, I do coke too. Sort of goes together. I used to deal weed, but that was in the old days and I never made any fucking money. I just did it to get my own gear for nothing.

'That's what we were talking about last night actually. The business about cannabis being made legit. Personally, I think it should've been made legal years ago like it is in Amsterdam. Although, it would put a lot of dealers out of business. Their profit will go down the toilet, unless they're big enough to be supplying wholesale. Because I think more people will smoke if it is legalized and that will increase demand. Supply and demand, simple economics. But the street dealer; forget it.

'But I got out of weed because I just wasn't making any money. It's not like I had a fucking job. I've never had one. Yeah, I've been a barman, stuff

---

In New York, heroin comes in $10 (£7) or $20 (£14) bags. In London it costs £10 ($15).

---

like that. I worked as a minicab driver once. But not a real job. So I needed cash and started doing a bit of nose. I met a few guys through that and got stuck into the smack. This was in the 1980s.

'To be honest I hadn't done smack before I started dealing, which I think is pretty unusual in this game. I done pretty much everything else: coke, spliff, speed, acid, loads of pills and thrills. So I had a little thing going with the cocaine. I was about the 100th fucking rung on the ladder, one up from the street basically, so about the time I got the stuff it was white powder, but there wasn't much fucking coke in it. It was cut with everything and I cut it further. I do the same now. I never put anything out pure. I got to make a profit.

'What happened was the guy I was getting my coke off gets shot. That was pretty unusual then. Now there's a lot of killing going on with crack, but this was a few years back and guns weren't so easy to come by. He was murdered. I can't even remember what his name is now. John, maybe.

A UK heroin user spends, on average, £8,516 ($12,340) each year on the drug.

He was shot in the neck and bled to death outside his flat. I don't know who did it or why, although I'm pretty certain it had something to do with the dealing. Maybe he hadn't paid his connection. I don't know.

'What I did know was where he kept his stash. It wasn't in his flat and once or twice he'd called me over to some lock up garages in Brixton. I don't know if he trusted me or something, but that is something you never fucking do. Let anyone in on your stash. Okay, it wasn't fucking hundreds of kilos. Maybe half a kilo [1lb], perhaps a bit more. I forget. But it was a fucking lot for me. And there was some other stuff there too. Ecstasy was getting big and he had bags of that. Hundreds of pills. Stereos, car shit and a whole bunch of other stuff in there that I ended up selling. I remember he had a stack of CDs; but it was the same fucking album by The Pogues. I had a hell of a job shifting that lot. I was knocking them out for about 50p [75 cents] around boozers before I offloaded the lot in Camden.

'As soon as I heard he was dead I went around the lock up and done it. We had to cut the door off in the end with a grinder, there were so many locks. But I got all his gear and the bent stuff and stuck it in a mate's car. I was fixed up then. It was a hell of lot of coke for me to get my hands on. I spend a whole day cutting it up with shit. I used to use anything that was white. Sugar, talc, aspirin, fucking anything. Sweets sometimes, travel sickness pills, flu powders, really fucking anything. I'd start off maybe making it 70 per cent pure. Then have a think. Cut it some more, down to 50 per cent. Give myself a line. Chalk it some more, down to 40 per cent or 30 per cent.

'I got all this coke, but I didn't have enough customers to get rid of it all. All my mates or friends of friends, you know, they were maybe getting a gram or two grams a week off me at most. So it would have taken fucking ages to get through that shit. I didn't know how to get rid of it. This was probably when coke was around £70 or £80 [$100 to $120] a gram. I could have brought my prices down, but people get suspicious if you're selling at £40 [$60] and everyone else is double that.

TOOLS OF THE TRADE

- Heroin
- Pager
- Mobile phone
- Car
- Kitchen or digital scales
- Balloons
- Black electrical tape
- Sandwich bags
- Talcum powder
- Ecstasy
- Laxatives

'I knew some of the guys that my connection worked with. I approached one bloke. I knew I was risking a lot because he could have been behind the killing or may have owned the coke I had, but I didn't have much choice. As it happens he wasn't too interested where I got the coke from. I think they were just looking for someone to fill the shoes of the dead guy so I got moved up the ladder. I was now selling stuff to street dealers. They put me in touch with a whole network that I got plugged into. They let me deal my own stash to start off, but I had to throw them back some money on anything I made. When I ran that down, which didn't take long, I got some more from them. I financed that with the coke I had sold. I was in. A real fucking dealer. That's what I do.

'Days are pretty much the same dealing. But what's good about heroin is the junkies want it all the fucking time. When I was doing coke people would get a wrap for the weekend, you know some advertising cunt or office worker wants to get high. Lick some coke off their girlfriend's tits. The rest of the time I'd be down the pub. But there's always someone who wants heroin – all the time, every day.

'What happened after I had been dealing in cocaine was that heroin started coming along. I would do a bit of work and then I found that I quite liked the junkies. They weren't like all the cunts trying to score coke. I didn't just supply, I started doing a bit of heroin. I'd not done any of it at this point. This is around the end of the 1980s.

'So I had a few bags. And I tried some. You know that expression? "Never get high on your own supply." It was meant for a reason. And that's smack, but I can't say it was my worst mistake. I just snorted it first off. I know most of the kids I was dealing to were smoking, some were injecting. But I hadn't got any works or anything then.

'I thought it was beautiful. Better than coke. Better than a lot of things and I'd done most of everything by then. I couldn't believe it and I couldn't believe it had taken me this long to get around to it. I kept dipping in and dipping in and dipping in until I was at it all the fucking time.

'I'd cut the stuff I was selling on even more. More smack for me. But it was still pretty good stuff and my habit didn't affect business. In fact it may have helped. You know junkies like dealing with other junkies, so I carved out a good little business.

'So now I've got heroin and coke and a habit. I'll usually pick up my heroin from my supplier today, Wednesday or Thursday. We don't like to be too predictable in this trade, but that's just how it works out. This guy brings it into the country. He's got a whole set-up with guys like me

ANATOMY OF A STREET DEAL
- Heroin addict calls the dealer
- Addict waits for the return call
- Dealer calls back and tells the addict where to be at a specified time
- Frequently used locations are car parks, busy streets or addict's home
- Addict waits
- Dealer is normally late
- Addict gets in to the dealer's car
- Dealer either remains parked or drives a short way
- Exchange occurs in the car
- Addict leaves the car and the dealer drives off
- The dealer and addict meet in the same way practically every day

taking shit off him to sell on, which is then sold on. I can be buying maybe £1,000 [$1,450] worth of gear each week. It's not all heroin, coke too and ecstasy. But I can convert that into £3,000 or £4,000 [$4,350 or $5,800] so the profit for me is fucking good. There's a lot of bigger dealers than me so they are doing fucking loads.

'I still deal to a small number of guys, though; ones who have been with me for years. I don't like letting them down and we're sort of mates now anyway. My phone normally starts to go off around lunchtime,

Convicted heroin smuggler Sandra Gregory walking to freedom after serving seven years of a 25-year sentence served when she was caught carrying heroin at Bangkok Airport in 1993. She was freed in 2001 when the King of Thailand granted her a royal pardon. Gregory had spent four and a half years at the notorious Lar Yao women's prison – dubbed the Bangkok Hilton – before she was repatriated in 1997 to serve the remainder of her sentence in Britain.

Michael and Pauline Holcroft, stepfather and mother of heroin addict Rachel Whitear, with the UK's Minister for Young People, Ivan Lewis (CENTRE), at the Department of Education in London. *Rachel's Story*, a graphic film made about Rachel's death from a heroin overdose, was made available to every school in the UK to warn pupils about the dangers of drugs. Rachel's parents also campaigned for longer jail sentences for dealers who deliberately target children.

sometimes a bit earlier. Junkies are always in bed 'til late, which suits me fine. I am too.

'I normally know them, so what I do is take the gear around. It's always the same places and it means I've never got the heroin at my place in case I get busted. I'm dealing in quantities of about half a gram to a gram, sometimes more. I sell a gram for £50 [$75] now, but I have done it for a lot less. It's still a lot cheaper than when I first got into the game though.

'I pick the smack up from a flat that is rented in the name of some fucker I picked out the phone book. It's a dump, but no one lives there. Just the dope. It's also in a really quiet street so no one is going to rob it. I never see anyone around, which is perfect. I don't need anyone getting too nosy.

'Once I've got it I'll drive around and drop off the dope. Most of these guys have got pretty strong habits. More than £100 [$145] a day. One guy has got a job. There's a girl who also works. The rest are on the rob, selling on stuff that I sell them or on the rock'n'roll [slang for 'dole': welfare].

'I never have anyone come around here. They can get me on my mobile most times. It doesn't take too long to spin around. Sometimes I may arrange a meet in a pub or club somewhere and sell the dope in the car park outside. Then there's walk-up trade. I'm always careful about that. You know it could be a copper and I've been caught out already.

'I don't think I look like a dealer. Actually, I don't fucking know. I've seen a lot of dealers. You know, professionals and they just look like your dad. It ain't like on TV where you've got some cool black guy with a load of gold jewellery, a great fucking car and a hot woman on his arm. White shag-pile carpets at home. Some of the guys I'm buying off, you wouldn't look twice at.

'But I guess I've got some stuff that I wouldn't ordinarily have. I've got a BMW for a start. A real giveaway, I suppose. I've got a house and a flat, on top of the flat I rent to keep my stash in. I always have a nice holiday. But the thing is I can't be away too long. If you're not around someone else is in, taking your business. I've got a sort of partner, who takes over my dealers when I'm off and I do his if he goes away. We operate in different patches of London so it's not like we are in competition and we also buy from the same supply, usually.

'But I don't live anywhere too flash. It's a nice house, in my wife's name, so she had better not leave me. I tell the neighbours I'm in advertising. I got that from all the fuckers I saw selling coke. They don't dress up too much and, from what I saw, never did any work. You know, it's supposed to be creative and they work abroad so it sort of adds up if I'm away or work strange hours. I say I was on a shoot. I don't think my neighbours have a fucking clue, but we don't live in each others' pockets. They're sort of professional people, lawyers and stuff, and don't get involved. I stick with my mates I've known ages.

'One time, about 15 years ago, I was in a club and got approached by a guy wanting ecstasy. He actually looked pretty good for an undercover cop. I think he might even have been on something. He was dancing, no shirt. The only thing that was strange was he wanted 20 ecstasy. He was really specific. Normally people would only need one or two for a night. Some bought for their mates so they might ask for five or six, but most kids just took one, even a half.

'Anyway, I thought "a sale's a sale" and got the stuff. If I was in a club I'd normally have someone with me who could get the gear in easily. Illegal raves were the best because no one bothered, but then they started getting doormen in when people collapsed. I got the 20 ecstasy for this guy and he goes off satisfied, or so I thought. But when I leave I get done by the cops. I know they weren't targeting me or anything. It was just a trawl of clubs and they got lucky with me that night. Actually, it could have been a lot worse. I didn't have a record or anything and they didn't know what else I was into. I played it like I was just doing my friends a favour holding their drugs. I got a suspended [jail sentence] for dealing. Touch wood, I haven't had any trouble since.

'To be honest I don't think the law is really after people like myself. They want to get the big, big fish. The guys running the smuggling, who set up all the dealers like me and the guys on the street. What's the point of closing us down? Someone else will just come along. But if they can break the distribution chain to the manufacturing high up then that's a result.

'But I don't go out of my way attracting attention. I've got a nice TV and we just had the kitchen done. The rest of the cash goes in the bank. I've got accounts in my own name, a few accounts in my wife's name. I even pay tax. I've got an accountant who I see once a year and thinks I work a window cleaning round. All cash, see. He must think I clean glass office blocks though. Obviously, I don't put all the money through this. But having a national insurance number, paying tax, it keeps me in the legit world.

'One thing about the dealing, though, is that I don't think I could give it up. Not just the heroin. I have tried to stop, but it's almost normal for me now to inject. Like I've got diabetes or something. It's not like I'm ever going to be in short supply. I'll inject this morning and then in the afternoon after I've done any business, picked up the gear or sold it on.

'But you get addicted to the trappings of the life. I remember when I was just selling weed. I was broke all the fucking time. It's just like gambling or doing drugs. Drug dealing is addictive. I know I wouldn't have a lot of the stuff I've got now with the drugs. I'm mostly off the streets so I'm not going to get picked up for that. And I'm not a major wholesale operator so there aren't going to be any undercover operations launched against me. Yeah, it works for me.

'I actually couldn't see me doing anything else now. Besides, I need to maintain my habit. One thing that sometimes gets to me is all the waiting around I do. You know you always hear from junkies that they have to wait for their connection. It's the same with me. I can arrange a meet to buy my supplies and get the runaround for an hour or more and this is from a guy I've known ten years. There is always a different place where the gear is brought in and stored. I just see the stuff I'm buying.

'It can be a bit fucking scary sometimes. Generally when I start thinking about what I'm doing. It could all turn to shit and I could be facing quite a bit of jail time. But I've seen most stuff; nowadays, really the only worry I get is from walk-ups turning out to be cops or nutters, or if I haven't got the money for my next week's supply. It's sort of a given that I will always offload a few grams, maybe 40 [1½oz] or 50 [1¾oz], each week. But no one wants to be stuck with a load of smack. As for most of the junkies, they're good as gold normally. Obviously, there's some that always try out for credit, but that doesn't work. No cash, no drugs. Simple as that.

'I've only had a couple of scrapes, nothing serious, though. If it was serious, chances are I wouldn't wake up from it. You know what I'm saying? But one funny thing was when I started selling to one bloke, a user in Chelsea. He was pretty well-off. I think his folks had died and left him the house and some money. He was quite posh, got a lot of fancy wines. He'd also been a rugby player so he was quite big.

'He had a little thing going on with some showbiz connections he had. I think it was a management company or some sort of agency for a lot of bands coming into the country. That lot always want drugs. Not always heroin, but one or two do it. I'd pass some gear on to him. I'd give him a good rate, lower than on the street, so he shouldn't have had any complaints.

'So I drop off some dope at this guy's place. A bit of coke and some weed and pills as well. He had some record label wankers there when I called around and wanted me to do some with him there and then with these fucking idiots. I think he had just started shooting up around then, but this had never happened before. He'd been good as gold, but I think he wanted to show off. Show the ponytails what a big man he was. Put Lou Reed on the stereo, you know the dealer has come around. But I made it a rule that I never do drugs with customers so I said, "No, I have to leave." But the cunt wouldn't have any of it and gets me in a neck lock. It was more ridiculous than anything else and we start scrapping in his front room. All the fucking drugs go all over the place and we're rolling around on his coffee table with these two wankers jumping out the way.

'I've got my supply for the week. What I do is cut it up before I sell it on to my boys. I used to have those crappy scales with weights and stuff, but now I got ones that they use in science labs. It cost nearly a £1,000 [$1,450] and it's ultra-sensitive with a digital readout. To tell you the truth, though, it's really all done with your eyes. People know how much a gram looks like, or a quarter. They might not know what the fuck is in there, but they can see if you're short-changing them.

'There's not much point in putting out crap bags. I've done it in the past, but you just get a bad name. I'm not saying I don't cut my gear up, but I ain't putting brickdust in there or anything that is going to kill someone. I don't want that on my conscience. It's normally headache pills I put in, crushed up, like. You know, I never know what I'm getting. You can sort of tell because I end up doing it and it's normally good stuff, but I ain't a chemist and I don't do an analysis on what I'm getting sold. Everyone knows this is how this trade works, though.

'In the afternoon I'm going around to about six places to drop off gear for some people. Three or four of them have already been on the blower checking that we're on. I know some who've got other dealers that they sometimes go to. It's like a security blanket for them. If one of us is out of town then they can turn somewhere else because there is nothing worse that not having a fix when you want a fix.

HOW TO SPOT A PROFESSIONAL DEALER IN THE NEIGHBOURHOOD

- His mobile phone is always ringing
- The size of his house is inconsistent with the job he claims to have
- He has lots of new, expensive gadgets
- He's at home a lot
- He makes many short car journeys
- He makes lots of visits late at night

'Then I'll meet with a few dealers who want to settle up for the weekend. I couldn't say how much they make. That's their business, but it isn't as much as everyone tells you. I know some who are just getting by, they get their own drugs free, but that's about it. These guys are where I used to be and are sort of at the end of a very long chain and all the sweetness is sucked out at the top end. I do all right, but it's a real shift up if I wanted to become a real wholesaler. I sometimes hear about guys getting caught in possession of kilos of coke or smack, and hundreds of thousands in cash – and I'm a little way short of that, and know I'm at the level I'm comfortable with. I've never been invited upstairs and I don't really want to go.

'The weekend is no different from any other day really. People still want junk and I put it out. My wife has got a couple of kids from a previous relationship. They're just five and seven now. A boy and a girl. We see them every weekend and I really enjoy that. Of course, they don't know what I'm doing or that I use. Nor does her ex. That would be like fucking...the end.

'So we do what normal couples do really with the kids. Walk around the park and stuff. Play football, nothing special. The cinema. I quite enjoy this part of it all, but I know I couldn't ever fit into the bit where I go to work and come home. The thing is, I'd like to have kids of my own, but there's no way while I'm on smack and dealing it.

'Sunday, I go to church. No, I'm joking.'

HEROIN LEGISLATION

Almost as quickly as drugs were introduced into society, laws were passed to limit their supply or – in more recent years – outlaw them totally. As long ago as 1729 the Chinese emperor Yung Cheng issued an edict prohibiting the smoking of opium and its sale, and in 1799 Kia King decreed poppy cultivation and its trade illegal.

In the West, the possession or supply of illicit drugs was largely not subject to prosecution until the middle of the 19th century when the 1868 Pharmacy and Poisons Act was introduced following a spate of fatal opium overdoses in Britain. But it wasn't particularly effective as it was based on self-regulation and users could still get opiates over the counter at pharmacies.

In the USA, controls were also lax and inconsistent until 1875 when San Francisco passed a law to prohibit opium smoking. In 1890, in its earliest law enforcement legislation on narcotics, US Congress imposed a tax on opium and morphine and, in 1906, Congress followed up with the Pure Food and Drug Act. This required contents labelling on medicines and other products containing opiates, and immediately cut the availability of opiates in drugstore powders and pills.

'The basic fact that eluded these great geniuses was that it takes only ten sq miles [16sq km] of poppy to feed the entire American heroin market, and they grow everywhere.' Myles Ambrose, former director of the US Office of Drug Abuse Law Enforcement 1972/73 on the futility of cutting the supply of opium

In 1909, US Congress passed the first federal drug prohibition law – the Smoking Opium Exclusion Act – outlawing the importation and use of opium. Then, in 1910, the Chinese, who had fought two Opium Wars – in 1839 and 1856 – with Britain in a bid to stop opium trafficking, finally persuaded the British government to dismantle the India–China opium trade and strictly enforce laws to restrict opium.

All modern global heroin legislation can essentially be traced back to 1909, when the first international Opium Commission was hosted by Shanghai. It focused primarily on opiate use in the Far East and countries with interests in that region and Persia were represented at the convention, which was chaired by Charles Henry Brent, the American Bishop of the Philippines, who became one of the most influential figures in combating drugs in the early part of the 20th century.

This conference laid the foundations for the International Opium Conference, held in The Hague in 1911. The British contingent, alarmed at the increased levels of smuggling in the Far East, proposed that the treaty should extend to the preparation and trade in morphine and cocaine. However, some countries – notably Germany – resisted this because they had huge pharmaceutical industries producing morphine-based drugs.

However, the conference did produce a treaty, the Opium Convention of 23 January 1912, which committed its 12 signatories to reducing opium and morphine abuse, and also the drugs prepared from them, which included heroin. However, in reality, the Convention went no further than obliging the countries to take measures to control the trade in opium within their own legal systems.

A second conference, held in The Hague in 1913, was equally unsuccessful at ratifying the Convention and halting the production of heroin. Although the German pharmaceutical company Bayer ceased production of the drug in the same year, heroin supply was out of control, with many cocaine addicts switching to the cheaper alternative. It was only at a third conference in The Hague in 1914 that a protocol was signed allowing the Convention to take effect.

The USA gave substance to this Convention in 1914 with the Harrison Narcotics Act. This was the first comprehensive control of opiates, which curbed heroin and cocaine abuse and addiction by requiring doctors, physicians and chemists to register and pay a tax. Illegal possession of substances named in the Convention also led to a maximum fine of $2000 (£1,380), five years' imprisonment or both. This also formalized the basis for the criminalization of the use of drugs in the USA for the next century.

The outbreak of World War I in 1914 interrupted further international law-making, though several European powers did move to tighten their border controls and domestic drug laws. For example, under a 1916 Spanish regulation, the sale of *medicamentos* was confined to prescriptions supplied at pharmacies, with stricter controls covering morphine.

The Netherlands also introduced an Opium Act in 1919 to outlaw opium-based drugs. However, by 1928, when possession was criminalized, the Dutch police often turned a blind eye and did not strictly enforce the country's drug laws.

In the UK, the government was worried about the uncontrolled supply of morphine and heroin throughout the armed forces and, in 1916, enacted Article 40(b) of the Defence of the Realm Act (DORA). This prohibited the supply of drugs, although not morphine, to army personnel and was later extended to encompass the whole country.

Following the end of the war and the signing of the Versailles peace treaty in 1919, the implementation of the 1912 international Opium Convention was made one of the conditions – Article 295 – of the peace deal. Responsibility for international narcotics legislation was put in the hands of the League of Nations and, in Britain, Article 295 became the Dangerous Drugs Act 1920.

This stipulated that only authorized bodies were allowed to manufacture or supply cocaine and opiates, such as morphine and heroin. Sales of drugs were logged and the Home Office began to regulate the import of opiates. Further legislation followed in 1923 with the Dangerous Drugs and Poisons Act, which amended the earlier Pharmacy Act.

In 1919, the League of Nations established the Social Questions and Opium Traffic Section and, by 1920, an Advisory Committee on Opium and other Dangerous Drugs was appointed. Britain, France (who in 1922 introduced a new law threatening ten years in prison for supply), The Netherlands, Japan, India, Portugal, and China all had permanent representation on this committee.

The climate for opium and heroin legislation was also influencing a wider world. In 1925 a new narcotic law in Egypt outlawed trafficking in drugs and the growing of opium poppies, and a few years later introduced the Central Narcotics Intelligence Bureau, following a sharp rise in the number of heroin addicts in Cairo's slums.

Despite opposition from some prominent physicians, who believed that heroin offered relief to patients, drug supplies in the USA were further controlled in 1922 with the Jones-Miller Narcotic Drugs Import and Export Act. And heroin was eventually outlawed completely in 1924, with the introduction of the Porter Act. This made the manufacture and use of the drug in medicine illegal.

This set a pattern for much of the resulting prohibitionist legislation governing heroin and opium supply over the next few decades, and demonstrated that the USA had not learned any lessons from the prohibition of alcohol: stamping out supply did not result in a downturn in demand. US narcotics agents, or narcs as they became known, from the Narcotics Division of the Prohibition Unit, were sent out to raid clinics and strangle the supply of legitimately produced medical supplies to addicts.

By 1923 the USA, which had not joined the League, began to attend Advisory Committee sessions and a further Opium Conference was opened in Geneva in November 1924. The first phase was directed at the issue of opium smoking with a second phase, two months later, aimed at curbing opium derivatives, especially heroin.

The US was represented at the conference by chairman of the House Foreign Affairs Committee Stephen Porter, who proposed the world prohibition of heroin. However, most participants believed that, while illicit supplies remained uncontrolled, complete suppression was impossible, and rejected his blanket ban. The US delegation walked out.

Despite the US walk-out at the Opium Conference, it passed a Convention that, in 1928, effectively put the control, manufacture, supply and sale of drugs in the hands of governments. Records on the levels of stocks of heroin and other drugs were ordered to be kept, and government departments took responsibility over their import and export.

The move had the effect of bringing into line the demand for legal morphine and heroin, required by legitimate hospitals and chemists, and the levels produced by licensed pharmaceutical companies. In the four years between 1928 and 1932, the global supply of 'legal' heroin fell by nearly 600 per cent.

In 1931, further conferences, which took place in Geneva and Bangkok, made efforts to suppress the illicit trade in narcotics and went further towards criminalizing the use of drugs by requiring all the Convention partners to introduce imprisonment for drug offenders. Restrictions were also placed on heroin, which at this point was being widely trafficked. However, with opium still being cultivated legally in the Far East, heroin use was not made a punishable offence at this stage.

A League of Nations convention for the Suppression of the Illicit Traffic in Dangerous Drugs followed in 1936, which made drug offences a crime punishable by extradition. A central office to supervise the prosecution of heroin and other drug traffickers was also established. Ironically, the USA refused to put its signature to the Convention because it did not include the trade in opium.

World War II also had the effect of mobilising the legislators. Concerned that its troops would become junkies, the USA forced through an agreement to outlaw opium smoking in the Dutch East Indies in 1943, and the British also agreed to stop selling opium in its territories. This meant that just a few years after the war, opium smoking had been outlawed everywhere in the world apart from Thailand, which eventually got around to banning it in 1959.

The United Nations took over responsibility for heroin and other dangerous drugs from the League Advisory Committee on Opium and Dangerous Drugs in 1946. The UN established the Commission on Narcotic Drugs, made up of 40 member states, and this began preparations for a worldwide drugs policy.

In 1948, the World Health Organization (WHO) was drawn into helping to formulate this policy and, in 1949, attempted to instigate a worldwide ban on the manufacture and use of heroin. That view got a good hearing in the USA where the Federal Bureau of Narcotics pushed for the compulsory imprisonment of drug users. The 1951 Boggs Bill also called for mandatory minimum sentences for opiate use and supply, ranging from between two and five years for a first offence and up to twenty years for third-time offenders.

The bill continued the momentum for more punitive overseas drug policies. The WHO recommended further drastic measures in 1953, when it called for all heroin production and imports to be wiped out. Then, in 1954, the UN pressed for the prohibition of the manufacture and trade in heroin unless it was destined for research or medical use.

The British government, fearing that a blanket ban on legally produced heroin would create a massive market of illicitly produced heroin, did not seek to ban heroin manufacture. However, it continued to restrict and control imports and exports of the drug. Also, in 1955, it did not renew licences for heroin production used in many cough remedies. Some other European countries, notably France and The Netherlands, followed suit.

The UN took over responsibility for heroin legislation worldwide in 1946.

The Boggs Bill was superseded by the 1956 Narcotic Control Act, which continued to pursue the USA's prohibitionist policies. Meanwhile, on the international stage, the UN introduced a single Convention on Narcotic Drugs in 1961. This replaced all previous Conventions and required all participating governments to restrict the trade, production and possession of narcotics to scientific and medical purposes. Any other activity was subject to punishment.

The Convention had four lists of substances, which were governed by a different regime of supervision. Also, on recommendations from the WHO, it could add new drugs to the lists if it could be shown that they presented a serious threat to public health or were involved in illicit trafficking. Depending on the degree of misuse, substances could be transferred between lists and national legislation would then be adapted to reflect the changes.

A series of laws was also introduced in the UK during the 1960s to act on drug abuse problems. These included the Drugs (Prevention of Misuse) Act 1964 and the Dangerous Drugs Act 1964, which ratified the 1961 New

York convention, and imposed the requirement for safe keeping and recording of heroin and other drugs.

In 1967 the Misuse of Drugs Act made it necessary for a UK doctor to be issued with a Home Office licence to prescribe heroin to a patient, and also gave the authorities powers to rescind that right. The act also introduced stop and search powers on a national level, giving police more tools to investigate misuse and dealing if they suspected someone was in possession of a controlled drug.

In response to America's growing drug problem, Congress passed the Controlled Substances Act of the Comprehensive Drug Abuse Prevention and Control Act 1970. It replaced more than 50 pieces of drug legislation and came into effect on 1 May 1971.

This law established a single system of control for both narcotic and psychotropic drugs for the first time in US history. It also established five schedules to classify controlled substances according to how dangerous they are, their potential for abuse and addiction, and whether they possess legitimate medical value.

The Misuse of Drugs Bill 1971 became the template for the UK's modern drug laws, which aim to balance legislation to stop abuse without restricting the correct use of drugs to help manage disease and pain. The bill consolidated various pieces of legislation dating back to the early part of the 20th century and provided heavier sentences for trafficking and lighter ones for possession.

CATEGORIZATION OF DRUGS

This bill outlined three categories (classes) of drugs according to their seriousness and awarded tariffs to punish offenders accordingly. Until 1985 it excluded barbiturates and still does not include other recreational drugs such as caffeine or amyl nitrate.

- Class A includes heroin, morphine, and opium.
- Class B includes codeine and dihydrocodeine; Class B drugs can be classed as Class A if injected.
- The least severe, Class C, includes benzodiazepine, mild amphetamines, and anabolic steroids.

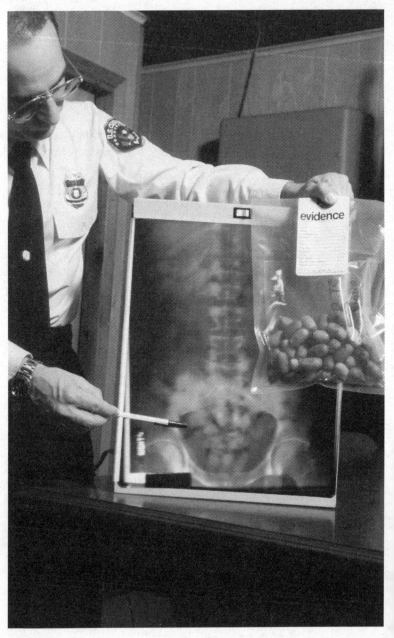

A New York customs official shows an X-ray of a drug smuggler's stomach contents. The bag (RIGHT) contains the recovered drugs.

Endoscope's view of several small bags of heroin found in the colon (large intestine) of a drug smuggler. The heroin is wrapped in plastic tape, each bundle around 2.5cm (1") long. One of these packets had burst inside the man's colon, causing him to lapse into a coma and stop breathing. After resuscitation, the packets were discovered on an X-ray.

13 bags of heroin removed from the smuggler's colon.

Further efforts by the UK government to stop heroin traffickers from profiting from assets gained in the illegal supply of the drug came about with the Drug Trafficking Act of 1994. This holds that, if a defendant cannot provide a reasonable explanation as to the source of his assets, they can be seized.

Governments worldwide have not always followed logical and productive drug policies, primarily because drug use has been perceived as a criminal activity and not a treatable problem. However, as the new millennium dawned and it became clear that purely prohibitionist policies had failed to cut the supply of heroin or the number of addicts, the voices – and arguments – calling for the legalization of heroin became more powerful.

DECRIMINALIZATION

Governments have now started to examine policies that allow some decriminalization or legalization and that would minimize the harm caused by drug abuse. The case for legalizing heroin begins with economists, who argue that any success in reducing the supply will raise the price of illegal drugs and cause more crime as addicts commit more burglaries or thefts to feed their habit. The resulting increase in profit margins earned by drug gangs will also spur them to greater efforts. The history of the drug trade is that supply always increases to meet demand.

In his respected 1994 book *Winning The War On Drugs: To Legalize Or Not?*, Richard Stevenson, an economist at Liverpool University, wrote that all drugs should be legalized, marketed and regulated so that they can be controlled. He described a scenario where large companies produce, distribute and market heroin, and invest heavily in research to make drugs safer: 'I am prepared to argue that drugs should be as legal as beer. They could be available from chemists clearly labelled and unquestionably with a government health warning.'

'Heroin itself is a highly dangerous substance, massively addictive and people take it, wind up becoming completely dependent upon it and wind up taking it with other substances as well and deaths are caused, in fairly large numbers.' Bob Ainsworth, UK Parliamentary Under Secretary for Anti-Drugs Coordination and Organized Crime, Home Office, giving evidence to the a 2002 drugs inquiry by a Home Affairs select committee

Stevenson and others suggest that the benefits of legalization would be avoiding the criminal acts attributed to the cost of maintaining the supply of the drug. Policing and legal costs would fall, as would the size of the criminal sector and the attendant strain on the legal system, saving the country millions. Legalization would pass heroin production, supply and profits from criminals to respectable tax-paying businessmen, and the government could earn millions. It is also likely that the price of heroin would fall by removing the legislation controlling it, which would leave the addict more money for food, clothing and to look after his health needs.

> 'Drugs are a tragedy for addicts. But criminalizing their use converts that into a disaster for society.' Milton Friedman, economist

This view has drawn wide – and sometimes surprising – support from a number of quarters, which argue that governments cannot control the supply and quality of drugs until they are in charge of things, and that treatment, rather than jail sentences, should be available for drug abusers.

Fulton Gillespie, parent of a heroin victim and a witness to the 2002 UK drugs inquiry by Chris Mullin's Home Affairs Select Committee, and whose drug experience are described in Chapter 3, argues that it is futile to try and stop young people taking drugs. He suggests that society has a greater responsibility to make drug taking safe. 'Those who believe legalization will make more hard drugs available to more young people overlook the fact that drugs of all kinds are more available to more young people now than ever, even with prohibition in force. There is not a whit of evidence to support the idea that there is some massive reservoir of disaffected youth about to rush out and die. There are more pushers out there than chemists' shops, so those who want to use hard drugs are using them now and will continue to use them, come what may,' he said.

In 2001, a call for a debate about legalization also came from certain sectors of the police. North Wales chief constable Richard Brunstrom published *The Drugs Debate: Time For Change?* in which he conceded that the war against the illegal drugs trade has failed, and also said that the attempt to control drugs' availability and supply had not worked. 'Proscription is not working,' he wrote. 'Drugs are ever more freely available...

There is no logic to the proscription list – alcohol and tobacco are our biggest killers.' His views were supported by former Gwent police chief constable Francis Wilkinson, who called for heroin to be legalized. He added, 'The current drug laws make the situation worse and any form of legalization would be preferable.'

In 2002 former UK government cabinet minister Mo Mowlam also argued that strict prohibition had not worked and called for the legalization of all drugs, including heroin. Mowlam said that the money raised from taxing drugs could be used for treatment. 'If the kids get hold of it because it's a high, they will get hold of it. Why not regulate it, take the tax from it, and deal with addiction?' she asked.

> 'A legalized, controlled, and regulated supply of heroin would reduce overdose deaths and enable users to live higher-quality lives and begin to deal with the problems that underlie their misuse.'
>
> Danny Kushlick, director of drugs reform agency Transform

TABLE 5.3: THE MISUSE OF DRUGS ACT, 1971 (UK)

CLASS A	The most dangerous and liable to the highest penalties Drugs covered include heroin and methadone Highest penalty for possession 7 years and life for supplying
CLASS B	Amphetamine sulphate, barbiturates, codeine Maximum penalty for possession 5 years and 14 years for supplying
CLASS C	Mild amphetamines, temazepam, and anabolic steroids, although some Class C drugs are legal to possess if they are in a medicinal form Penalty for possession is 2 years and 5 years for supply

UK HEROIN OFFENCES
POSSESSION

A person has heroin under their control; but supplying a person who is legally entitled to have the drug is not an offence. Possession of heroin in the UK will result in six months' imprisonment, a £5,000 ($7,270) fine, or both, in a magistrate's court. In a crown court, penalties are more serious at seven years, an unlimited fine or both.

POSSESSION WITH INTENT TO SUPPLY

The amount of heroin is not always relevant and even giving a small bag to a friend for safe keeping falls under this charge. If the friend returns the bag, he will also be found guilty of supply. If the amount seized in a person's possession appears to be more than for personal use that might also be used as evidence of intent. Evidence of scales, cutting equipment and bags, used in the wholesale supply of heroin, will also be used by the prosecution. In a magistrate's court, possession of heroin with intent to supply could earn six months' jail time, a £5,000 ($7,250) fine or both. In the crown court, the person could be sentenced to life or be required to pay an unlimited fine.

USE OF PREMISES

If a householder allows his premises to be used for the consumption of heroin, then he or she is liable to between six months' and 14 years' imprisonment and a fine of £5,000 ($7,250) or more.

The Misuse of Drugs Act regulations divide controlled drugs into five schedules, which list drugs according to who may lawfully produce, trade and handle them:

- Drugs in Schedule 1 include heroin and are the most stringently controlled because they can only be supplied or possessed with a Home Office licence;
- Drugs in Schedules 2 to 4 are available for medical use, but are normally controlled by a prescription – temazepam, for example, is listed under Schedule 4 and can be possessed if it has been prescribed for medical use;
- At the other end of the scale, Schedule 5 drugs can be sold over the counter at chemists.

LEGISLATION AROUND THE WORLD

AUSTRALIA

Heroin production and importation were prohibited in 1953 by Commonwealth legislation.

AUSTRIA
The Narcotics Law, 1951, originally allowed consumption of narcotics. But in 1985 tighter legislation was introduced and the Methadone Act 1987 now regulates methadone substitution.

BELGIUM
The Ministry of Interior, Ministry of Justice and Ministry of Health divide up crime prevention, legal and criminal areas, and drug prescription monitoring. Providing syringes for the illegal consumption of drugs is a crime.

BULGARIA
Several laws were passed in the early 1970s to restrict and prohibit drug trafficking and consumption. Anyone testing HIV positive is obliged to report for a medical.

CZECH REPUBLIC
Restrictive drug laws were introduced after the Velvet Revolution in 1989, although heroin is still cheaper here than in Western Europe.

DENMARK
Danish law makes no distinction between hard and soft drugs, and needles are sold from vending machines in Copenhagen and other cities.

FINLAND
The Care of Substance Abusers Act, 1985, enforces the use of compulsory treatment where applicable. Possession and use of drugs is illegal.

FRANCE
No distinction between hard and soft drugs. Severe penalties for trafficking and most prosecutions are for possession, not use.

GERMANY
Germany's Drug Act has three levels of categories for narcotics:

completely forbidden (which includes heroin); strictly regulated and not acceptable to prescribe; and strictly regulated, but can be prescribed medically.

ITALY
An action plan to consolidate the country's fight against drugs came into force in 1990 with a law on drug dependence.

IRELAND
Possession for personal use is punishable with up to seven years for hard drugs, and a fine and up to three years for soft drugs.

LATVIA
No distinction between hard and soft drugs.

LITHUANIA
No distinction between hard and soft drugs. Drug use could result in a prison sentence of between 15 days and 24 months, depending on number of convictions. Trafficking punishable with prison terms between 6 and 15 years.

LUXEMBOURG
Heroin users can be compelled to undergo compulsory treatment.

THE NETHERLANDS
No police action to detect offences involving the possession of drugs for personal use. No legal restrictions on the distribution of methadone or the sale of syringes.

NORWAY
Crimes against the country's Drugs Act are liable to heavy fines, with a maximum prison sentence of 21 years. A tip-off telephone line was introduced in 1990 to enable the public to inform on heroin or other drug dealers.

POLAND
Poland's Drug Abuse Prevention Act 1985 includes obligatory treatmenl for users under the age of 18.

PORTUGAL
Heroin traffickers and users face prison sentences. Syringes are available free under a needle exchange programme.

ROMANIA
Drug laws were passed in 1969 and 1979 to regulate the production, possession and circulation of narcotics.

RUSSIA
In 1998, the liberal Federal Law on Drugs and Psychotropic Substances, which made a distinction between the dealer and consumer of heroin, was replaced by a new Federal Law. An amount of heroin exceeding 0.005g is now punishable by a prison sentence of up to 15 years.

SPAIN
Distinguishes between hard drugs and soft drugs. The sale of syringes is permitted.

SWEDEN
Generally, drug policy is repressive and restrictive, and the maximum sentence for a drugs-related offence is 14 years.

UKRAINE
Still governed by tough laws from the Soviet regime. Syringes are not widely available.

UK
The principle legislation is Misuse of Drugs Act 1971, which divided drugs into three categories (Class A, Class B and Class C) according to their degree of harmfulness. Heroin is a Class A drug.

FIRST PERSON

INTERVIEW WITH BOB AINSWORTH, UK PARLIAMENTARY UNDER-SECRETARY FOR ANTI-DRUGS COORDINATION AND ORGANIZED CRIME, HOME OFFICE, MAY 2002

Q: Why is heroin perceived to be such a pernicious drug and where does it rank in the UK government's anti-drugs strategy?

AINSWORTH: Heroin is the drug that is most commonly associated with drug-related death. Death can occur as a result of respiratory depression, aspiration of vomit, pulmonary oedema or acute allergic reaction. It is also highly addictive. For these reasons, heroin is a Class A drug and a focus for the government's anti-drugs strategy.

Q: The government has been criticized for relying too heavily on legislation and law enforcement to fight the problem of heroin. What other tools are available and how do you think they will be effective in stopping the supply of drugs and the numbers of addicts from increasing?

A: We are clear that for our drugs strategy to work effectively – that is to stop the damage caused by the misuse of drugs – we need to proactively fund treatment and prevention services alongside work to enforce our drugs laws and stifle supply.

We know treatment works. We know that interventions, like arrest referral schemes and drug testing and treatment orders, help break the link between drugs and crime, thereby helping individuals and communities. The criminal justice system provides a unique opportunity to get drug users to address their problems and steer them into treatment and away from offending and, equally importantly, break their association with the illegal drug market.

Over time, we want our provision of treatment and prevention services to be so successful that the activities that demand enforcement are significantly reduced. We can only truly break the cycle of drugs and crime if we are in a position to offer a way out through treatment, thereby removing the customers that feed the supply market.

We have been reviewing the treatment available to opiate addicts. The main body of evidence demonstrates the value of methadone mixture for the majority. However, heroin prescribing is a valuable supplement to other treatment modalities, although clearly not a substitute. The government will not be making pharmaceutical heroin available to all current opiate addicts – this would lead to problems of continued injecting behaviour, and has the potential for increasing and prolonging the heroin-injecting population. However, we do want to ensure that all those who could benefit from heroin prescribing have access to it.

In February [2002] we held a consensus event of experts – including UK, Swiss, and Dutch representatives – to look at heroin prescribing. Some of the key points agreed were:

- that heroin prescribing is appropriate for patients who do not respond to methadone and psycho-social treatments – a minority of heroin addicts;
- improved access and availability of methadone treatment is a key prerequisite to enhanced heroin prescribing;
- the development of services for the supervision of heroin use is essential for any expansion of heroin prescribing;
- the National Treatment Agency should publish updated guidance on heroin prescribing by December 2002.

Q: The Home Office is reviewing the ten-year strategy put in place by former drug tsar Keith Hellawell in 1998. Why is it doing that and what are its new objectives likely to be in relation to heroin?

A: It was always planned that, three years into the strategy, the targets would be reviewed to make sure they reflect the current position. The targets were set in June 1999 at levels that reflected the US and Australian targets, as these were the appropriate benchmark at the time. Significant progress has been made since then in setting up programmes, and additional funding has been provided for services and research. That is why we are currently undertaking a stocktaking review. We are looking hard at the structure of the strategy, its balance and focus, the targets and progress *against them. Also, as part of the Treasury's Spending Review 2002, we are looking at the resources needed to take the strategy forward over the next three years.*

I cannot say, yet, what the outcome will be. The level of funding will be announced during the summer [2002], as will the results of our stocktaking review. However, in the context of heroin, we know we need to continue to focus on Class A drugs, which cause the most harm, and to do more to tackle problematic drug use. We need to focus more on harm reduction and breaking the link between drugs and crime, providing more effective help to those whose drug-taking causes serious damage to their own lives, to their families and to their communities. These are not radical changes – more a refocus, building on what works and filling in gaps.

Q: Some countries and experts have proposed decriminalizing heroin. Could you ever envisage a time when heroin's status as a Class A drug in this country would be downgraded or decriminalized?

A: Heroin is the drug that is most commonly associated with drug-related death. Death can occur as a result of respiratory depression, aspiration of vomit, pulmonary oedema or acute allergic reaction. It is also highly addictive. For these reasons heroin is a Class A drug and a focus for the government's anti-drugs strategy.

Those that argue against our drugs laws point to the costs of the criminal justice system and the costs of criminal involvement in the supply of illegal drugs. But rarely do they seek to balance these against the other costs to society of drug misuse; the costs of treating addiction and the enormous range of acute and chronic health problems; the cost to the individual, the family and the community.

We know that our laws deter experimentation and the level of use. For example, the MORI opinion poll for the Police Foundation Inquiry showed that 30 per cent of adults cited illegality as the main reason for not taking drugs; 64 per cent of respondents to the Youth Lifestyle Survey in 1998/99 gave the same answer in respect of cannabis. We must be clear that our drugs laws cannot eliminate drug misuse, but they do help to limit it. If we agree that this must be a key goal for society, how would legalizing drugs and stimulating demand by increasing their supply and driving down prices achieve this goal? Our drugs laws are the background against which the many and varied elements of our strategy are given the opportunity to work.

Q: Several countries have also experimented with different schemes that give addicts free access to heroin in controlled environments. What is the government's opinion of this and would it consider providing similar 'shooting galleries'?

A: The International Narcotics Control Board, in its 1999 Annual Report has indicated that the development of injection rooms contravenes international treaty obligations. The current government position is that injecting rooms for illicit drugs should not be introduced in this country whilst we have no evaluations of those developed in other European countries. We would only consider contributing to any evaluation through the World Health Organization in view of the uncertain legal status of injecting rooms. We would not wish to consider any research initiative that could cause the UK to undermine the UN Conventions as that would not set a positive example to other signatories.

Q: The 'Heroin Screws You Up' advertising campaign in the 1980s and recent photographs of the addict Rachel Whitear generated a lot of publicity, but many experts say that these 'shock tactics' don't work. Do you believe that is true and what role, if any, can the media and advertising play in future anti-heroin strategies?

A: The effect of an appeal using personal experience from the loved ones of a drug use victim needs to be fully evaluated. Coming from the government, the use of shock tactics can cause fear and alarm among children who are least likely to experiment with drugs, but can stimulate interest among those most likely to take risks.

The first stage in determining whether advertising could play a role in future anti-heroin strategies would be to conduct research with a representative cross-section of the target audience in order to discover:

- *whether communications/advertising could play a role*
- *what strategic approaches would work best*
- *what creative routes or ideas are likely to have most impact.*

If it was thought that advertising could play a role, initial creative ideas (scripts, design ideas etc) would then be pre-tested with the target audience using qualitative research in order to confirm that the advertising will have the desired effect. Only once this has been established would any creative work actually go into production.

Good drug education should teach young people about the dangers and harmful effects of drugs. It should also teach young people the skills and knowledge [they need] to make decisions about a healthy lifestyle and resist drug misuse in order to achieve their full potential in society.

Q: Drugs are estimated to cost the government at least £2 billion [$2.9 billion] each year in terms of crime, policing, and health treatment. How much does the government estimate heroin contributes to that figure?

A: The annual economic cost of Class A drug misuse is between £3.7 billion and £6.8 billion [$5.4 billion and $9.9 billion]. Problematic drug use accounts for almost all economic costs (99 per cent). Just over 80 per cent of problematic drug use is associated with heroin use, and 81 per cent of problematic drug use is associated with poly-drug use. Economic costs are therefore mostly associated with heroin use but also with poly-drug use. Costs by individual drug use are not usually estimated, and are likely to be influenced by a range of other important factors.

Q: Drug experts are predicting a major influx of heroin on to UK streets over the next 12 months. What measures are the government taking to prevent that?

A: Customs have put in place an end-to-end strategy to interdict drugs along the supply chain. They have a network of drug liaison officers working in key countries along the heroin route and also provide help and technical assistance to these countries. Western pressure will continue in the same vein and law enforcement agencies will continue to gather intelligence and react accordingly to the threat presented.

Customs and its partners have plans in place to combat opiate trafficking from the Afghan region. We hope that peace in the region and the new government will provide opportunities for us to assist with drug enforcement and, with other agencies, help prevent the resurgence of poppy cultivation.

HEROIN CRIME

As soon as drug laws were introduced, handling heroin became a crime, and criminal gangs grew to profit from it. Like the alcohol-banning Volstead Act 1919 in the USA, which heralded a decade of Prohibition and created criminal gangs willing to supply bootlegged booze, the introduction of tougher drug legislation in the USA and Europe led inexorably to control of the heroin business by organized crime.

DRUG-RUNNING

The American smugglers John Cushing and John Jacob Astor had already made vast profits from shipping Turkish opium to Canton in the 18th century after poppy cultivation in China had been banned. But the new drug laws of the early 1920s were seen as a new opportunity for a new breed of gangster: the drug runner.

One of the first and biggest American drug traffickers was Arnold Rothstein, who had made a fortune from gambling, illegal liquor and Prohibition dens such as the notorious Cotton Club. Almost as soon as the Jones-Miller Narcotic Drugs Import and Export Act 1922 and the Porter Acts were in place, Rothstein's and others' gangs were shipping opiates and cocaine back to the USA from Europe.

'70 per cent of crime is drug related.'
Action on Addiction, 2002

The drugs were cut and distributed stateside and the criminals' success was illustrated by a sixfold increase in the amount of narcotics seized by US Customs in just one year, from 1925 to 1926. Organized crime and the smuggling of heroin exploded alongside the new prohibitionist policies, sponsored by the USA and followed by Europe, during the 1920s.

The earliest drug racketeers included the Frenchman Henry de Monfreid in Europe and Africa and, in the USA, the Jewish gangster Meyer Lansky, the mobster Lucky Luciano, a hired hand of Rothstein who had been arrested in 1916 for dealing in heroin, and Jack 'Legs' Diamond, another Rothstein employee suspected of killing a New York heroin courier in 1928.

They set the rules, ruthlessly enforced them and became the prototypes for the cold-blooded, but hugely profitable Turkish, French, and Corsican heroin drug gangs that emerged in the 1970s and were followed by the Colombians and Mexicans a decade later.

> 'The global drugs trade is almost certainly the world's largest illicit market. It has been estimated by the UN Office for Drug Control and Crime Prevention to be worth in excess of $400 billion [£276 billion] per year.' Chief Constable Richard Brunstrom

The injured of World War I increased the number of morphine – and later heroin – addicts and as demand for drugs rose, illegal supplies also increased. Initially illicit heroin found its way on to the illegal drug market following break-ins at pharmaceutical manufacturers. However, opiates were also supplied from legitimate drug companies with the Allied occupying forces in Germany and across Europe providing well-trained traffickers of heroin and morphine.

The British banned Hoffmann-La Roche's products throughout its empire in 1925, although lifted the control a year later after the Swiss group introduced a system of controls on exports. But leaks of heroin, which found their way on to the illicit market, came from other European drug companies, and secret illicit laboratories were also set up to take over the supply of opiates and heroin.

In Britain, Assistant Under Secretary of State, Sir Malcolm Delevingne, urged the elimination of traffickers as the only way to cut out heroin and other drug users. Similarly, the USA was taking steps to stop the international traffickers. An international network was set up in 1930 to catch the gangs, with US agents spread through Europe and working with British and French drug enforcement units.

The problem with breaking the gangs was that the supply and production of opium had increased. India had always been an important producer of opium, but Persia became an increasingly important exporter of poppies to the Far East, Russia and Europe in the 1920s. The opium was turned into heroin in illegal labs set up in Japan and throughout Asia.

Opium was also available in China and opium gangs quickly sprang up to supply illicit heroin in this region and Hong Kong, which became a magnet for organized crime gangs in the 1930s. In the early years of heroin manufacture and trafficking, the Balkans also became an important crime centre. Bulgaria, Serbia, and Turkey all produced opium poppies, and European and Japanese traffickers set up heroin factories in cities such as Constantinople.

By 1930 poppy growing was being phased out in India, and Turkey had assumed the mantle of the world's major heroin producer. Istanbul became a magnet for French and Japanese illegal producers and traffickers, and by the mid-1930s it was estimated that over 72,000kg (65 tons) of heroin was being manufactured in the city.

France also had its problem with illicit heroin manufacturers, who bought opium in Turkey, processed it into heroin and supplied the drug to the USA and the Far East. And in Bulgaria, which was party to the Geneva limitation agreements, opium poppy cultivation multiplied in the early part of the 19th century, with illicit heroin factories established in Sofia.

In Japan, mercenaries were used throughout the 1920s and 1930s to help traffic the illicit heroin that Japanese pharmaceutical companies were manufacturing, for supply mainly to China. By the mid-1930s the Japanese army gave protection to drug traffickers in China, and the government actually encouraged opium growing and the supply of narcotics like heroin to overseas countries as part of its foreign policy to help colonize parts of the Far East. By the start of World War II, Japan was the world's biggest supplier of heroin.

Opium and heroin traffickers also emerged in Russia, where Manchuria became an important centre for shipping illicit drugs. In Germany and Austria, pharmaceutical companies were also manufacturing more morphine-based drugs than domestic supply warranted and much of it found its way into criminal hands. US trafficker Arnold Rothstein often bought directly from Berlin factories, although the rise of Hitler and the Nazi Party clamped down on leakages.

In the same way as the Opium Exclusion Act 1909 had caused an increase in the illegal trade in heroin, a 1925 crackdown on opiates in Egypt also helped increase the use and supply of heroin. Switzerland was also a notorious supplier of morphine and heroin, which was sometimes smuggled inside clocks or boxes of chocolates, or disguised as less harmful drugs.

Tough drug laws also encouraged drug trafficking in Latin America in the mid-1920s. Chile, Argentina, Peru, and Honduras all became major centres for gangsters dealing in opium, morphine and heroin. Some couriers employed fake certificates to get around the limitations imposed by the League of Nations and also used the practice of diplomatic immunity to bypass customs.

Illegal heroin labs had first been discovered near Marseille in 1937. These labs were run by the legendary Corsican gang leader Paul Carbone. For years the French underworld had been involved in the manufacturing and trafficking of illegal heroin abroad, primarily to the USA. Marseille's convenience and the frequent arrival of ships from opium-producing countries made it easy to smuggle the morphine base, but its prominence as a major centre for heroin export was sealed in the late 1940s when the US Central Intelligence Agency (CIA) armed and funded Corsican gangs in their opposition to French communists.

THE FRENCH CONNECTION

Corsican gangs took control of the French port's illegal trade in opium and heroin and, by the early 1950s, it was a major link between the Sicilian Mafia and US heroin users – this was the 'French Connection'. This new phase in the development of heroin crime came when the USA unwittingly helped traffickers by linking them to the Mafia in Sicily.

In 1946, America deported hundreds of gangsters, including Lucky Luciano, whose experience and expertise in the heroin trade interested Mafia bosses in Palermo. The Mafia began buying opium. They mostly bought from Turkey, whose farmers were licensed to grow opium poppies for sale to legal drug companies, but sold their excess to the underworld

> The UK government spends around £1.4 billion ($2 billion) on drug-related activity, approximately 62 per cent on enforcement

market. The Mafia also opened heroin labs in Marseilles and Sicily to process the heroin and then smuggle the drug to US and Canadian cities.

The first significant post-World War II seizure was made in New York in 1947, when 3kg (7lb) of heroin were seized from a Corsican seaman disembarking from a vessel that had just arrived from France. In 1949, more than 23kg (50llb) of opium and heroin were seized on the French ship *Batista*, but the first major French Connection case occurred in 1960 when an informant told a drug agent in Lebanon that Mauricio Rosal, the Guatemalan Ambassador to Belgium, The Netherlands, and Luxembourg, was smuggling morphine base from Beirut to Marseilles. In one year alone, Rosal had used his diplomatic status to smuggle about 200kg (440lb) of smack.

The French traffickers continued to exploit the demand for their product and by 1969 were shipping to the United States between 80 to 90 per cent – around ten tonnes of heroin – of all its heroin supply. The heroin they supplied was also very good, approximately 85 per cent pure. The French Connection continued into the 1970s, but was finally cut following a 1971 political coup in Turkey, which saw a new regime willing to ban opium growing in return for US aid.

NEW ROUTES
With the fall of the French Connection new supplies were needed to satisfy the USA market, and Mexico helped fill the gap with the rise of Latin

smugglers shipping across the Texan and Californian borders. At about the same time the Mafia was being joined by Cuban gangs in importing heroin into the USA. Cubans had begun settling in Florida following the disastrous 1961 Bay of Pigs invasion, but further criminal immigrants arrived over the next two decades, including thousands of criminals deported by Fidel Castro.

Further illegal heroin supplies followed another disasterous US foreign policy intervention. The CIA began to give assistance to the Chinese Nationalists in the 1950s. Unfortunately, they trafficked in opium. In the following decade, the CIA pumped arms into Laos near the border with Vietnam to support Hmong tribesmen in resisting communism. Again, the anti-communist's main source of funding was the opium poppy and these heroin warlords expanded opium production by pledging that the money raised would help fight communism. The CIA was even complicit in helping move the opium to labs in the Golden Triangle (Myanmar, Laos, and Thailand), and heroin was shipped to Vietnam and other countries in the region.

During the Vietnam War, some 10 per cent of US soldiers were thought to be heroin users and until the US withdrawal from Vietnam in 1973, it is thought that about one-third of the illicit heroin that washed up on the streets of US cities came from the Golden Triangle labs the CIA had helped set up.

In 1979, US President Jimmy Carter began helping the Mojaheddin guerrillas in resisting the Soviet occupation of Afghanistan. However, like the tribesmen in Laos, the Afghan fighters grew and sold opium poppies to help finance their war. By 1980, over half of the heroin flooding into the USA was from Afghanistan and the country remains the world's largest illicit opium producer, with a proliferation of heroin factories in Pakistan.

The war in Kosovo in 1999 also inadvertently led to Europe being flooded with smack. Following the NATO bombing campaign, which forced Serbian forces out of the ethnic Albanian province, the region became a centre for smugglers unfettered by law enforcement. Agencies estimated that some 40 per cent of the heroin sold in Europe and North America was flowing through the province in 2000, with the traffickers handling up to five tonnes of heroin each month compared to around two tonnes before the conflict.

The links between heroin and crime were made startlingly clear in 2001 when UK Home Office research showed that 29 per cent of all arrestees tested positive for opiates or cocaine, and that about one-third of the proceeds of acquisitive crime went back towards buying heroin or crack.

Partly as a result of these findings, the UK shifted its emphasis on tackling criminals to targeting the profits they make through heroin. Marking the introduction into Parliament of the Proceeds of Crime Bill, which was designed to dismantle and disrupt criminal gangs, Home Office minister Bob Ainsworth said, 'Criminals should not be allowed to profit from their crime. Crime barons make their money off the back of local communities' misery. They cash in on the illegal drug markets, burglary, and muggings that plague innocent people's lives.'

The UK trade in illegal drugs is estimated at £6.6 billion ($9.6 billion).

By 2002 the UK's law enforcement agencies also admitted that they had adopted the wrong strategy – of focusing resources on individuals and seizing heroin shipments – for drug crimes. It was also reported that they had accepted they did not know about 60 per cent of the drug trade.

In a radical shift, UK police and customs accepted that their future approach would concentrate on choking off the profits of traffickers: chasing profits, not powder. One tactic was to mount covert surveillance on suspected *bureau de change* outlets, which are used by drug gangs to launder money.

HEROIN TRAFFICKING METHODS
THE SEEDS OF SMUGGLING

Heroin's journey to the streets of New York, London, or Paris begins with the planting of the opium poppy. Around three months after the poppy seeds have been planted, the milky opium sap is harvested, and the dark brown gum shaped into bricks or cakes and wrapped in plastic.

These are sold by the farmer to a dealer, who will probably have a morphine-refining plant – nothing more elaborate than a few drums and a stove in a rudimentary lab – close by. The opium brick will be mixed with lime in boiling water until a band of morphine forms on the surface and can be drawn off; it is then reheated with ammonia, filtered, and boiled again until reduced to a brown paste.

The morphine base, with the consistency of modelling clay, will be poured into moulds and dried in the sun ready for further processing into heroin. This may take place in another illicit lab, albeit a more sophisticated one.

When the heroin emerges from these labs it enters a complex chain of distribution. Large dealers will usually deal in shipments of anything up to several hundred kilos, which will then be divided into smaller packages of between 1kg (2¼lb) and 10kg (22lb) for sale to street gangs. These will be split

It is estimated that only 10 to 15 per cent of illegal heroin is ever intercepted by law enforcement agencies.

further into bags of a gram or less for sale to users. The number of street dealers in a given area can vary enormously and will depend on the number of heroin users present, police activity and even the area's historical status as a drug-dealing centre. King's Cross in London and the East Village in New York, for example, have reputations as places to cop.

SUPPLYING DEMAND

The more the law enforcement measures are upgraded, the more complicated the drug traffickers' modus operandi become. In the course of the struggle against drug trafficking, anti-drug control forces have been faced with a wide spectrum of concealment methods.

Typically, different drug gangs will control cultivation and production levels, and regulate prices. At the wholesale level, however, the trafficking process becomes more diversified and can involve a number of different smuggling groups and brokers. Brokers will often have close connections with a several rival producers, and heroin traffickers form limited partnerships with different groups to ensure business flexibility, continual supply, and a measure of protection from the law.

CONCEALMENT METHODS

Heroin moves from the region of source and production to the consuming markets by a variety of methods, usually involving either air, sea or land, or a combination of these. Heroin smugglers have been forced to be more creative because trafficking laws are increasingly stringent, and police and customs officials are devising new ways to detect drugs.

It is a challenge traffickers are rising to. New techniques are seemingly limited only by a trafficker's imagination and are being helped by new technology. However, invariably the most effective methods are the simplest. Air and sea remain the principal methods of transporting large amounts of Southeast Asian, Afghan, and South American heroin to markets such as the USA and Europe. The high volume of commercial air and maritime traffic provides a natural camouflage for heroin concealed in containers, and multiple port transfers help obscure the origin of the illicit cargo.

COURIERS AND MULES

Trafficking groups also use couriers, or mules, to smuggle small amounts of heroin, usually up to 2kg (4½lb), on commercial air flights or through border crossings in private cars or on foot. The mules conceal the heroin in their luggage, body cavities or stomachs by drug swallowing. This is one of the commonest and most dangerous methods of concealment; the narcotics are packed in small multi-layered plastic bags. Despite the danger of these being torn up in the stomach, the mules are paid very little.

In Liverpool, during the early 1990s, Dr John Marks used a special Home Office licence to prescribe heroin to addicts. Police reported a 96 per cent reduction in acquisitive crime among a group of addict patients.

Other, more imaginative and bizarre, ways of smuggling heroin through customs are always being tested and, in February 2002, one mule flying into a Florida airport was stopped after it was discovered that a Colombian laundry had starched all his shirts and jeans using over two pounds of heroin. Customs inspectors stopped the mule after noticing the unusually stiff clothes that smelled of vinegar and left a trail of white powder. Another border patrol in Texas uncovered $5 million (£3.5 million) worth of narcotics stuffed inside the body parts – legs, arms and intestines – of a stolen corpse. The traffickers used the body to disguise the scent of the drugs from sniffer dogs.

Criminal groups supplying the USA from South America or from Mexico often use the land route through the southwest border with Texas. Illegal immigrants and migrant workers smuggle between 1kg (2½lb) and 3kg (6½lb) loads, but larger amounts are delivered by truck.

Mexican heroin distribution networks in the United States are managed almost entirely by criminal

The annual consumption of pure heroin in Britain is running at between 28,000kg and 36,000kg (25 tons and 32 tons).

organizations operating from Mexico and by Mexican-American criminal gangs that are in charge of the street-level distribution of heroin. Groups from the Dominican Republic have also played a significant role in retail-level heroin distribution using bases in east-coast cities, including New York, Boston, and Philadelphia.

In Afghanistan and neighbouring countries like Pakistan and Iran, less sophisticated, but by no means less successful, modes of heroin transportation are used. These can include jeep, motorbike or even camel caravans, which can carry up to seven tonnes of narcotics. The advantage of these methods is that there is no need for smugglers to accompany the caravan, which can be controlled by traffickers operating from remote mountainous areas.

Trafficking organizations employ drug distribution network and creative marketing techniques to expand the heroin market in the country they are supplying. There have been instances of some gangs providing free samples of heroin to traditional cocaine or other drug buyers in order to attract new custom.

During the smuggling process the weight and the bulk of the drug is kept to a minimum and heroin is handled in as highly concentrated a state as possible, often with a purity exceeding 90 per cent. Before sale, it is diluted several times. The substances used for adulteration vary considerably, but include fenacetine and methaqualone, which have intoxicating properties themselves.

Southeast Asian heroin traffickers typically deal in 700g (25oz) units, in contrast with South American, Mexican, and Southwest Asian heroin traffickers, who traffic in kilogram quantities. When produced in refineries in Southeast Asia, heroin is usually packaged in half-unit blocks (350g [12oz] per block) of compressed powder. These rectangular blocks are 2.5cm (1in) thick and measure 13 by 10cm (5 by 4in).

CONTAINERIZED CARGO

Because of the huge volume of worldwide commercial trade and the necessity of containerized cargo, heroin traffickers continue to employ commercial containerized cargo on aircraft and merchant ships as a successful smuggling method.

For example, heroin processed in the Golden Triangle (Myanmar, Laos, and Thailand) is smuggled overland to Myanmar, China, Thailand, Malaysia, and Vietnam for transhipment by air or sea within containerized cargo through Taiwan, Hong Kong, Singapore, Japan, and Korea. From these transit countries, the heroin is shipped to consumer markets in Europe, Australia, Canada and the USA.

Many similar characteristics are common among containerized-smuggling heroin trafficking gangs. They include renting or buying import/export companies or warehouses within the source and transit countries, such as Thailand and the USA, for the sole purpose of smuggling and storing drugs. Heroin traffickers will frequently change the names of these 'front companies',

Heroin is smuggled in as highly concentrated a state as possible, often with a purity exceeding 90 per cent.

but they sometimes maintain the same addresses and will remain as long as the companies have not themselves been compromised.

Typically, one entire 8m (20ft) or 16m (40ft) container is leased and filled with a cheap range of goods. Popular lines for heroin smugglers are plastic bags, soy sauce, T-shirts and chopsticks; however, gangs often use seafood and other perishables as a way of discouraging customs inspection.

Usually the commodity is packed in cardboard cartons of uniform size and weight, and stacked on pallets. The cartons containing the heroin are placed deep within the container. There may be only one pallet that contains all the cartons of heroin, or single cartons of heroin may be placed among the individual cartons of the commodity, but as a rule fewer than ten cartons of heroin will be concealed within around 1,000 cartons of the commercial cargo.

Concealment methods in the cartons also vary. For example, the heroin may be placed in cans that are weighted the same as the canned commodities or the heroin may be formed into the shape of the items in the cartons. Traffickers will also add weights in an attempt to minimize differences between those packs containing heroin and those that don't.

In 2000, a kilogram (2¼lb) of heroin cost $2,700 (£1,863) in Pakistan and $129,380 (£89,272) in the USA.

Drug-laden cartons will also be marked or numbered to distinguish them from the legitimate commercial cargo cartons. For example, a woman's image was stamped on one shipment, and the boxes containing the heroin were identified by shading in one of the woman's eyes.

Containers will also be insured for up to ten times more than the actual value of the commercial cargo and, in many cases, heroin shipments will transit a secondary port prior to shipment to the final destination to put officials off the trail. For example, heroin produced within the Golden Triangle may be shipped to secondary ports in Taiwan, China, Hong Kong, Malaysia, Singapore, Tokyo, or South Korea. A new bill of lading will be issued to indicate that the cargo originated somewhere other than the Golden Triangle.

HI-TECH SMUGGLING

New technologies are also increasingly being used by the heroin smuggler. In its 2001 Annual Report, the International Narcotics Control Board (INCB) highlighted its concerns about the misuse of new technologies in international drug control. The board said that drug-trafficking groups utilize new technologies, such as the Internet and electronic pocket organizers that can store contact and bank account details, sales records and coordinates for landing strips, to improve the

Sgt Keith Hughes of Edmonton Police Station, north London, with a haul of high-quality heroin with a street value of over £8 million ($12 million) and weapons seized in a series or raids in 1996.

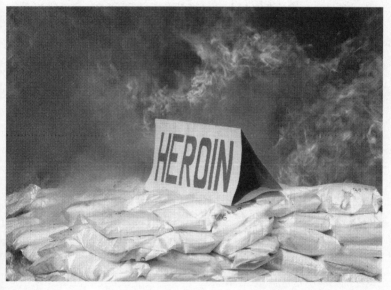

As part of the Fourth Interpol Heroin Conference in 1999, Myanmar authorities destroyed 4,023kg (8,869lb) of opium, 431kg (950lb) of heroin, 33kg (73lb) of morphine, 28kg (62lb) of marijuana, and 15.4 million tablets of stimulants.

efficiency of heroin's delivery and distribution. Drug traffickers were also using computers to conceal information about drug shipments by using encrypted messages, and to protect themselves and their illicit operations from investigation by drug law enforcement agencies.

WHAT HEROIN CRIME COSTS

Trafficking costs money to fight, but there are a number of other links between heroin and crime. Addicts often resort to burglary, shoplifting, fraud or other theft to support their habit. This contributes a large share of the cost to a country through the damage or loss of property, the cost of replacing it and insurance.

However, heroin and crime can also be linked in a number of other ways and will also add to the total crime bill. Some people will be caught in possession of, or supplying, illegal heroin. This will add to law enforcement, police and court time and costs.

Further crimes, ranging from manslaughter to driving offences, may also be committed while under the influence of heroin. Violence between rival gangs of heroin dealers, or between a dealer and a dependent user, will also count towards the crime figures and costs.

UK police forces estimate that around half of all recorded crime has some drug-related element to it. Drug-related crime is costing the criminal justice system at least £1 billion ($1.45 billion) every year.

Finding out how much heroin crime costs is a very complex process, however, and little or no consensus has been reached. In the USA, annual economic costs related to drug abuse were estimated to be $110 billion (£76 billion) a year, or 1.5 per cent of GDP in the mid-1990s (UN drug report, 2000), but the many estimates that have attempted to find out the 'cost of crime' element have pitched figures anywhere between $1 and $3 billion (£0.7 billion and £2 billion).

Similarly, in the UK, attempts have been made to accurately assess the size of the illegal market in heroin and also the cost of drug-related crime and, specifically, how much heroin contributes to the bottom line of the UK bill.

UK researchers have suggested that there are between 130,000 and 200,000 problematic drug users in the UK, committing theft and other crimes to support habits costing each of them up to £30,000 ($43,500) annually. However, since stolen goods only fetch about one-third of their value, the total cost of stolen goods could be up to £2.5 billion ($3.6 billion) each year.

Further research about the cost of heroin abuse on society was revealed in 2002 when research by the University of York was presented by Bob Ainsworth, Parliamentary Under Secretary of State at the UK's Home Office with responsibility for Anti-Drugs Coordination and Organized Crime. It showed that drug abuse in England and Wales costs society up to £18.8 billion ($27.2 billion) a year with hardcore heroin and crack cocaine addicts responsible for some 99 per cent of that bill (it estimated

'Just one kilo (2¼lb) of heroin distributed at street level can generate 220 victims of burglary and £220,000 [$320,000] worth of property stolen by addicts to fuel their habit.' Bob Ainsworth, Parliamentary Under Secretary of State for Anti-Drugs Coordination and Organized Crime, Home Office

that there were 281,125 heroin or cocaine users whose 'habits were no longer under control' and that they are each costing the state around £30,000 ($43,500) a year, or £600 ($870) each week).

Furthermore, the research stated that the UK's National Health Service spent £235 million ($341 million) on doctor services, accident and emergency admissions, and other treatment linked to drug abuse. When these health service costs are added to the criminal justice system and the welfare state, costs rise to between £3.7 billion and £6.8 billion ($5.4 billion and $9.9 billion). However, with the addition of social costs the bill rises to between £10.9 billion and £18.8 billion ($15.8 billion and $27.2 billion).

ADDITIONAL INFO

SUMMARY

For the past few decades, the world has been fighting a war on heroin, but with many countries using only the limited weapons of legislation and punishment, few have managed to isolate the enemy, let alone slay it. Most have tried to reduce the user population, only to see it rise. They have tried to strangle the supply, only to see it increase and heroin prices fall. And they have tried to inflict casualties on crime gangs that profit from heroin, only to see them proliferate and get richer.

It seems that almost every effort to wipe heroin from the face of the planet has failed. The policy makers in many countries are now at an important crossroads and face a tough question: Will they persist in fighting a principled but ultimately ineffectual campaign against heroin, or do they accept that the war cannot be won and opt for living with the drug while putting in place systems and treatment to minimise its effects on users and society?

It appears that most westernized countries are now acknowledging the fact that, if there is one single lesson to be learned from the experience of the last 30 years, it is that policies based on enforcement are destined not to succeed. The best that the world's lawmakers can claim to have done is partly to stem heroin's spread. At worst, they have simply created new problems of organised crime. Therefore, the reduction of harm rather than retribution seems to offer a more effective way of dealing with the problem.

As Chris Mullin, chairman of the UK's Home Affairs Select Committee, which in May 2002 published one of the most far-reaching reports on drugs in Britain, said, 'We have to face the fact that, whether we like it or not, large numbers of young people take drugs. As far as users are concerned, our priorities should be realistic education, readily available treatment, and harm reduction. Above all, we have to focus on that relatively small minority of drug users who are making a misery of their own lives and those of others.'

With this in mind, it appears that more countries are now willing to pick up and use new tools to combat heroin and its abuse, and some have signalled their intention to follow the lead set by countries such as Australia, the Netherlands and Switzerland, who have adopted progressive drug measures and taken a more enlightened approach to the ways in which they tackle the problem of heroin. In due course, these new ways of reaching and treating the heroin addicts who cause most damage to themselves and others will include looking at the efficacy of prescribing heroin – which would undercut the illegal heroin market and drug-related crime – and the provision of 'shooting galleries' – safe-injecting rooms – which would take the most chronic addicts off the street.

These and other new methods will also be tried and tested – and, in some instances, discarded – over the next decade as evidence is gathered to back up their use. However, in the long term, as costs are met and political and social resistance is overcome, it is likely that more harm-reduction treatments will move automatically from the pilot stage to being nationally or universally adopted. In some countries, use of these methods may even require changes in law to allow pharmacists to supply drug users with relevant paraphernalia in order to reduce the risks of heroin use, such as swabs, citric acid, and needles.

At the same time, the future success of moves to deal with heroin lies in better education with a view to stopping users from taking up heroin in the first place. Drugs are increasingly part of most young people's lives and it's essential that the world's governments get balanced, accurate information about them across to their young. However, the area is under-resourced and there is still a huge and unresolved debate over the effectiveness of many of the drug campaigns that have been used to reach teenagers and educate them. Few have moved on radically from the rhetoric of the 'just say no' tactics, where education was based on fear rather than knowledge. Indeed, there is evidence that these warnings may actually stimulate drug experimentation. And there have been fewer still campaigns aimed solely at heroin.

Today's youth knows that one puff on a joint doesn't lead inexorably to a full-blown heroin addiction, so drug education messages need to accept that reality and ensure that messages are credible if kids are to listen to them in the first place. This means that, if the war against heroin is not winnable in absolute terms, then at least it will claim fewer casualties.

HEROIN WEBSITES

www.drugs.gov.uk – UK government information and statistics on drugs

www.drugscope.org.uk – Leading UK independent centre of expertise on drug information and policy

www.nta.nhs.uk – The UK National Treatment Agency

www.eata.org.uk – European Association for the Treatment of Addiction

www.emcdda.org – European Monitory Centre on Drugs and Drug Addiction

www.usdoj.gov – Contains information about heroin from the US Department of Justice Drug Enforcement Administration

www.drugs.indiana – Heroin information; also explores the glamorization of heroin by celebrities and in popular culture

www.heroinpages.org – Information about heroin addiction, substance abuse and how to get help; comment forum, needle exchange and rehab

www.drugstory.org – Informational resource on illegal substances, including heroin

www.heroin.org – Information on opium, morphine, and heroin

www.herointimes.com – An online magazine about heroin and heroin addiction

www.drugfreeamerica.org – Drug resource with information about heroin

www.heroinabuse.net – Heroin tolerance, addiction, withdrawal

www.heroinkills.com – Anti-drugs site

www.drugtext.org – Includes heroin information

www.drugpolicy.org – Facts about heroin in US cities

www.cia.gov – US law agency facts on heroin movements worldwide

www.who.int – World Heath Organization statistics and information on substance abuse

www.heroin.co.uk – Includes discussion on heroin literature

www.undcp.org – UN drug facts, reports and latest figures on worldwide heroin and drug abuse

www.doh.gov.uk – Statistics on young people and drug misuse in England

www.homeoffice.gov.uk – UK government figures on smoking, drinking and drug use among young people

STREET NAMES FOR HEROIN

Al Capone	Caca
Antifreeze	Capital H
Aries	Charley
Aunt Hazel	Cheese
Ballot	Chieva
Bart Simpson	China white
Beast	Chinese red
Big bag	Chip
Big H	Crown crap
Big Harry	Deuce
Birdie powder	Diesel
Black pearl	Dirt
Black stuff	Doa
Black tar blanco	Dog food
Blows	Dogie
Blue bag	Dooley
Bombido	Dope
Bombs away	Dr Feelgood
Bonita	Dragon
Boy	Dreck
Bozo	Duji
Brain damage	Dyno
Brick gum	Dyno-pure
Broja	Eighth
Brown	Eldiablo
Brown crystal	Estuffa
Brown rhine	Ferry dust
Brown sugar	Foo foo
Brown tape	Foolish powder
Bundle	Furra
Butu	Galloping horse
Caballo	Gallup

Garnot

Gear

George

George Smack

Girl

Glacines

Golden girl

Golpe

Good H

Good horse

H caps

Hache

Hairy

Hard candy

Hard stuff

Harry

Hazel

Heaven dust

Helen

Hell dust

Henry

Hera

Hero

Hessle

Him

Hombre

Horse

Horsebite

Hot dope

HRN

Isda

Jee gee

Jerry Springer

Jive

Jojee

Joy

Joy flakes

Joy powder

Junco

Junk

Kabayo

Mexican brown

Mexican horse

Mexican mud

Mojo

Mud

Murotugora

Muzzle

Nanoo

Nice and easy

Nickel bag

Noise

Number 4

Number 8

Nurse

Ogoy

Old Steve

Orange line

P funk

Pack

Parachute

Peg

Perfect high

Poison

Poppy

Powder

Predator

Primo

Pure

Quill

Racehorse Charlie

Rambo

Raw fusion

Rawhide

Red chicken

Red eagle

Red rock

Reindeer dust

Rhine

Sack

Salt

Scag

Scat

Scate

Scott

Shit

Shoot

Silk

Skag

Skid

Sleeper

Slime

Smack

Spider blue

Stuff

Sweet dreams

Sweet Jesus

The beast

The witch

Thunder

Tits

TNT

Tongs

Tootsie roll

White

White boy

White junk

White nurse

White stuff

Witch hazel

JUNKIE SLANG

AIP – heroin from Afghanistan, Iran and Pakistan

Atom bomb – heroin mixed with marijuana

Back to back – smoking crack after injecting heroin

Bad bundle – low-quality heroin

Bag – pack of heroin

Ball – Mexican black-tar heroin

Balloon – heroin dealer or balloon containing heroin

Belushi – cocaine and heroin

Bindle – small pack of heroin

Blank – non-narcotic powder passed off as heroin

Bomb – very potent heroin

Channel swimmer – someone who injects

Chasing the dragon – crack mixed with heroin, smoking heroin

Chase the tiger – to smoke heroin

China cat – very pure heroin

Chipper – occasional user

Chocolate chip cookies – MDMA mixed with heroin or methadone

Chocolate rock – crack smoked with heroin

Chucks – hunger following withdrawal

Cigarette paper – packet of heroin

Cook – to mix heroin with water; heating to prepare for injection

Cook down – to liquefy heroin in preparation for inhaling it

Cotton brothers – heroin, cocaine, and morphine

Crap – low-quality heroin

Criss-crossing – snorting up lines of cocaine and heroin simultaneously

Crop – low-quality heroin

Deck – between 1g and 15g (½oz) of heroin

Dime's worth – amount of heroin that would cause death

Dinosaurs – old users or addicts

Dragon rock – mixture of heroin and crack

Dust – to add heroin to marijuana

Dynamite – cocaine mixed with heroin

Eightball – crack mixed with heroin

Five way – snorting heroin, cocaine, methamphetamine, and crushed flunitrazepam pills, and drinking booze

Flamethrowers – cigarettes laced with heroin and cocaine

Flea powder – low-purity heroin

Foil – baking foil used to cook up and smoke heroin

Frisco special – heroin, cocaine and LSD

Frisco speedball – heroin, cocaine and a small amount of LSD

Garbage – inferior heroin

Get-off houses – places where users can buy and inject

Give wings – inject someone or teach them how to inject

Glass – hypodermic needle

Goofball – heroin mixed with cocaine

Gravy – to inject heroin

H&C – heroin and cocaine

H-bomb – heroin mixed with ecstasy

Half load – 15 bags of heroin

Half piece – 14g (½oz) of heroin

Homicide – heroin cut with scopolamine or strychnine

Hong yen – heroin in pill form

Horning – to inhale

Hot heroin – poisoned heroin

Hype – addict

Jolly pop – casual user

Jones – addiction

Karachi – heroin, phenobarbital, and methaqualone

LBJ – heroin, LSD, PCP

Lemonade – poor-quality heroin

Load – 25 bags of heroin

Meth speedball – methamphetamine mixed with heroin

Moonrock – heroin mixed with crack

Mortal combat – very pure heroin

Murder one – heroin and cocaine

New jack swing – heroin and morphine

This Is **HEROIN**

Nod - using heroin

One-on-one house - place to buy heroin and cocaine

One-plus-one sales - selling heroin and cocaine together

P dope - 20-30 per cent pure heroin

Paper - a small dose of heroin

Paper boy - dealer

Polo - mix of heroin and motion sickness drug

Primos - cigarette laced with cocaine and heroin

Ragweed - poor-quality heroin

Red rock opium - heroin, barbital, strychnine, and caffeine

Red rum - another name for heroin, barbital, strychnine, and caffeine

Rider - 5kg (11lb) of free heroin on top of a 100kg (220lb) shipment of cocaine

Sandwich - heroin between two layers of cocaine

Scramble - heroin cut with other drugs or non-narcotics

Serial speedballing - doing cocaine, cough syrup and heroin continuously over a couple of days

Shooting up - injecting

Smoking gun - heroin and cocaine

Sniffer bag - £3.45 ($5) bag of heroin intended for snorting

Snowball - cocaine and heroin

Speedball - cocaine mixed with heroin; crack with heroin smoked together; methylphenidate
    mixed with heroin

Speedballing - shooting up or smoking cocaine and heroin

Spike - heroin cut with scopolamine or strychnine; to inject; needle

Spoon - 1.75g ($\frac{1}{16}$oz) heroin; used to prepare heroin

Tar - crack and heroin smoked together

Taste - small sample of drug

Tecatos - Hispanic addict

Twists - small bags of heroin

Whack - heroin and PCP

Whiz bang - heroin and cocaine

Wicked - very pure heroin

Z - 28g (1oz) heroin

GLOSSARY

Agonist – A compound that will bind to a receptor and create a pharmacological response.

Analgesic – A drug that reduces pain. Analgesics act on the brain; opium derivatives such as morphine are powerful, but easily produce addiction. Non-narcotic analgesics, of which paracetamol and anti-inflammatories (such as aspirin) are the most common, act peripherally by preventing the formation of pain-producing substances, and are effective for headaches and minor pains.

Antagonist – A compound that will bind to a receptor to form a complex that does not give any response.

Codeine – Found in opium, but this mild to moderate painkiller is usually synthesized from morphine in medical products. Known on the streets as T-Three, cough syrup and schoolboy.

Drug – Any chemical substance that alters the physiological state of a living organism. Drugs are widely used in medicine for the prevention, diagnosis and treatment of diseases; they include analgesics, anaesthetics, antihistamines and anticoagulants.

Endomorphin – Two endogenous peptides that function as mu-agonists.

Endorphins – A peptide that functions as a selective agonist for the mu-opioid receptors.

Heroin – Heroin, or diacetylmorphine, is a narcotic compound that is a synthetic derivative of morphine. The compound is easily absorbed by the brain, and is used as a sedative and powerful analgesic. Very addictive.

Morphine – Naturally occurring substance in the opium poppy. Called M, morph and Miss Emma on the streets, it is a potent narcotic analgesic.

Narcotic – A drug that induces drowsiness, stupor or insensibility. Narcotics include the opioid and synthesized compounds with morphine-like properties. They are powerful analgesics, used in medicine.

Opiate – One of a group of drugs derived from opium, an extract of the poppy plant that depresses brain function (a narcotic action). Opiates include morphine and its synthetic derivatives, such as heroin and codeine.

Opioid – Any one of a group of substances that produces pharmacological and physiological effects similar to those of morphine. Opioids are not necessarily structurally similar to morphine, and include fentanyl and methadone.

Papaver – A widely distributed, summer-flowering annual somniferum plant: *Papaver somniferum*, of the poppy family, Papaveraceae. It is grown in hot, dry climates for the drug opium, which is extracted from its sap. The raw material is refined to produce heroin.

This Is **HEROIN**

Partial agonist – A compound that possesses affinity for a receptor, but will produce only a small pharmacological response.

Semi-synthetic – A compound with some opioid receptor similarities, synthesized by modification of product extracted from opium and including heroin.

Synthetic opiate – A compound with some opioid receptor similarities but using no material extracted from opium. Includes methadone.

TIMELINE

c3400 BC: The opium poppy is cultivated in lower Mesopotamia by the Sumerians, who would later pass on their poppy culling art to the Assyrians

c1300 BC: Egyptians begin cultivation of poppies in Thebes, and the opium trade flourishes under Thutmose IV

c1100 BC: Opium harvested on Cyprus

c460 BC: Hippocrates recognizes opium's use as a narcotic and for treating diseases

330 BC: Persia and India are introduced to opium by Alexander the Great

300 BC: Arabs, Greeks and Romans begin to use opium as a sedative

AD 400: Arab traders introduce opium to China

1300-1500: Opium becomes taboo and disappears from Europe for 200 years

1500: Portuguese traders begin the practice of smoking opium

1527: Laudanum painkillers, which contained opium, introduced to Europe

1606: Elizabeth I orders ships to transport Indian opium back to England

1680: Thomas Sydenham combines opium, sherry and herbs to produce Sydenham's Laudanum, which becomes a popular remedy for various ailments

1689: Tobacco is mixed with opium in East Indies opium dens

1700: Indian opium exported to China and Southeast Asia by the Dutch, who introduce the practice of smoking opium with a tobacco pipe

1729: Chinese emperor Yung Cheng prohibits opium smoking

1750: The British East India Company (BEIC) takes control of the Indian opium growing districts of Bihar and Bengal; Britain dominates the trade in opium between Calcutta and China

1767: The BEIC imports 2,000 chests of opium to China, most for medicinal use

1780: British traders establish an opium depot at Macao

1793: Indian poppy growers are only allowed to sell opium to the BEIC, which gains total monopoly over its trade

1796: China bans the import of opium, but illegal trade continues

1799: Opium poppy cultivation in China is banned

1803: Friedrich Sertürner discovers morphine, the active ingredient of opium, after dissolving it in acid and neutralizing it with ammonia

1804: Opium trading resumes at Canton, despite 1799 edict

1805: American smuggler Charles Cabot attempts to smuggle opium into China

1812-16: Opium smuggling becomes big business with trade between Turkey and Canton

1819: Writer John Keats and other literary figures, such as Byron and Coleridge, indulge in recreational use of opium

1821: Thomas De Quincey publishes *Confessions Of An English Opium Eater*

1827: The German pharmaceutical company, E Merck & Co, starts to manufacture morphine in commercial quantities

1832: Codeine extracted from opium

1839: The start of the first Opium War between Britain and China

1841: Britain defeats China, which cedes Hong Kong

1843: Dr Alexander Wood uses syringe to administer morphine

1852: British introduce Indian opium to Burma

1856: Second Opium War with China

1874: English researcher CR Alder Wright first synthesizes heroin; smoking opium banned in San Francisco

1878: Opium Act passed in Britain, which restricts the sale of opium to registered Chinese opium smokers

1890: US Congress imposes a tax on opium and morphine

1895: Working with morphine at the German company Bayer, Heinrich Dreser produces diacetylmorphine (heroin) and Bayer begins commercial production

1905: US bans opium

1906: Britain and China move to restrict the Sino-Indian opium trade; the US Pure Food and Drug Act requires medicines to label contents

1909: International Opium Commission in Shanghai

1910: Britain dismantles the opium trade between India and China

1914: Harrison Narcotics Act in USA, which requires pharmacists and doctors who prescribe heroin and other narcotics to register and pay tax

1923: US Treasury Department's Narcotics Division bans all narcotic sales, leading addicts to turn to illegal sources

1945: Burma gains independence, and opium cultivation and trade flourishes

1948: Corsican gangsters begin their illegal assault on the US market with heroin refined from Turkish opium in Marseille labs

1950s: US foreign policy aimed at containing the spread of communism in Asia (by financing and arming drug warlords in the 'Golden Triangle' – Myanmar, Laos, and Thailand) unwittingly increases production and flow of heroin

1962: Burma outlaws opium

1965-70: The number of heroin addicts in the USA estimated at around 750,000

1970: Controlled Substances Act passed in USA, divides drugs into groups and establishes penalties; the USA creates the Drug Enforcement Administration (DEA)

Mid-1970s: A new source of raw opium found in Mexico's Sierra Madre, which introduces 'Mexican mud' to US cities

1978: Opium fields in Mexico are sprayed with Agent Orange in a massive joint anti-drug initiative by the US and Mexican governments; drug smugglers turn to new supplies of opium from the 'Golden Crescent' – Iran, Afghanistan, Pakistan

1988: Opium production increases in Burma under the State Law and Order Restoration Council junta

1992: Colombia begins shipping high-grade heroin to the USA

1993: The Thai army and US DEA cooperate on destroying opium fields in the Golden Triangle

1995: The Golden Triangle becomes the world's biggest opium producer, with annual yields of 2,500 tonnes

1996-2002: Heroin trafficking continues to be problem with involvement of Chinese, Nigerian, Mexican and Colombian crime organizations

INDEX

217

Mankind has chewed it for thousands of years, has snorted and smoked it for centuries, and has now refined it to reach the brain in under four seconds. Its chemistry sustains Peruvian hill farmers and sharp-suited banking professionals alike, and it is the fastest growing recreational drug – 6.6 million Americans (3 per cent of the entire US population) take cocaine weekly and a recent survey of British 16–24-year-olds revealed that 50 per cent had used it. The social and scientific arguments swirling around it get denser by the year. Everything about it defies simple analysis. It brings euphoria and despair, obscene wealth and dire poverty. It knows no social barriers.

Frank and unbiased, *This Is Cocaine* looks at the drug's curious history, the extraordinary world of drug lords and traffickers, and the politics of its production. Above all, it explains the science of cocaine addiction, the health implications, and ways in which users can minimize the risk of using it.

If you're doing cocaine, or you know someone who is, *This Is Cocaine* is essential reading.

ISBN 1 86074 423 0

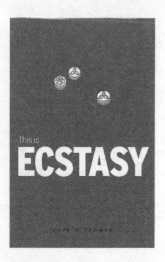

Ecstasy is a problem child. One of the most notorious designer drugs to have risen out of the '80s rave scene, a young drug embraced by the young, the stuff of peer pressure rather than caution. An official survey estimates that in the UK 430,000 users spend a total of £300 million ($441 million) a year on ecstasy, taking between one and five pills a night, while unofficial sources have it that consumption is twice this figure. To date, there have been around 90 E-related deaths reported in the UK and around 40 in the United States, where E is no longer just a club drug but is increasingly available in schools and homes, finding new customers in ex-cocaine users.

This Is Ecstasy presents the very latest information from around the world concerning the drug's culture, manufacture, and trafficking, its medical origin (it was once nicknamed 'penicillin for the soul'), its short- and long-term effects on health, the legal and political ramifications of its use, and the consequent backlash from supporters of the drug.

In the words of Alexander Shulgin, the remarkable scientist who nurtured ecstasy through its infancy, 'Be informed, then choose.'

ISBN 1 86074 426 5

This Is
CANNABIS

In the 4,700 years since its first recorded use, cannabis has been respected as a highly useful source of fibre, food, and medicine and vilified as a social menace. Society in the 21st century seems to be of both opinions: doctors and scientists spend millions exploiting its medicinal value and thousands of people travel to Amsterdam each weekend to sit in cafés to smoke copious amounts of dope free from molestation, yet taking less than 30g (1oz) back into their own countries is an offence and public figures who admit to smoking cannabis in their youth claim that they did so without inhaling.

This Is Cannabis does not preach the benefits or the deficits of cannabis; instead, it aims to provide the facts about cannabis in an authoritative, straightforward way, outlining the history, laws, and culture that have accreted around it, its effects on health, and the booming commercial potential.

ISBN 1 86074 399 4

Also available
in this series